JUL 17 1997

D1559626

BETWEEN
GENEALOGY
AND
EPISTEMOLOGY

Todd May

BETWEEN GENEALOGY AND EPISTEMOLOGY

Psychology, Politics,
and Knowledge
in the
Thought of Michel Foucault

The Pennsylvania State University Press
University Park, Pennsylvania

Library of Congress Cataloging-in-Publication Data

May, Todd, 1955–
    Between genealogy and epistemology : psychology, politics, and
knowledge in the thought of Michel Foucault / Todd May.

        p.   cm.
    Includes bibliographical references and index.
    ISBN 0-271-00905-5
    1. Foucault, Michel.   I. Title.
B2430.F724M39   1993
194—dc20   92-29112
                                                                    CIP

Published by The Pennsylvania State University Press, Suite C, Barbara Building,
University Park, PA 16802-1003

Printed in the United States of America

It is the policy of The Pennsylvania State University Press to use acid-free paper for the
first printing of all clothbound books. Publications on uncoated stock satisfy the mini-
mum requirements of American National Standard for Information Sciences—Perma-
nence of Paper for Printed Library Materials, ANSI Z39.48–1984.

CONTENTS

For Kathleen and David

ACKNOWLEDGMENTS

I would like to thank Alphonso Lingis, Joseph Flay, Robert Corrington, and Conrad and Kay Pritscher for careful readings of and helpful suggestions for the manuscript. I would also like to thank Joseph Margolis and Joseph Rouse, both of whom provided detailed commentary on earlier versions of the text. Sanford Thatcher and Charles Purrenhage made the process of review and editing much easier than it would otherwise have been.

There are two people to whom I owe an irredeemable intellectual debt: Mark Lance and Panos Alexakos.

Above all, I would like to thank Nancy Love for unfailing encouragement and guidance.

1

MICROPOLITICS

Near the end of his life, Michel Foucault often referred to a small text of Kant's, "What Is Enlightenment?" (Kant 1963). It seems that this little piece had marked a path along which, two hundred years later, Foucault would find himself traveling. There is a profound power that, if his statements are to be believed, Foucault ascribes to this note of Kant's. He says it is the text that inaugurates "a form of reflection within which I have tried to work" (Foucault 1986c, p. 96). That form of reflection, which passes through Hegel, Nietzsche, and the Frankfurt School, is obsessed with a single question, one that remains the same although the answer constantly changes: What is our present?

To ask about our present, to ask what it is, is not so abstract a question as it may appear. For what Foucault is after in holding this question to be the organizing principle of his life's work is neither an ontology nor a metaphysics. It is not a matter of delving into the Being of the present, but rather of asking the more pedestrian and yet more urgent question: What are things like for us today? In what kinds of situations do we find ourselves, in what kinds of predicaments and with what kinds of troubles? What are the constraints that (immediately apparent to us or not) bind us, the oppressions that beset us? And how did we let all this happen?

Many answers can be given to the questions posed to us by our present, and there are many avenues by which to approach those questions. In his life, Foucault chose three avenues, which correspond roughly to the three periods into which his work is generally divided: archaeology, genealogy, and ethics. Although all are addressed to the present and our attempt to understand it, these avenues have more in common than that very general orientation. They are all concerned to articulate, in different regions of our present, "how the human subject entered into *games of truth*" (Foucault, in Bernauer and Rasmussen 1988, p. 1). For Foucault, the questions of what we hold to be true and how we came to do so, especially as regards ourselves, are of paramount importance in attempting to articulate an understanding of what our present is.

The significance of these questions is not confined to their relevance for comprehending our situation. In fact, what is at stake in the questions of what we hold true and how we came to do so is the conduct of our lives. How we understand what we have come to accept about the world and about ourselves, the context in which we place our various knowledges of things, determines not only the theoretical underpinnings of our epistemology but also the political and ethical commitments of our practice. Both the knowledge that Foucault attempted to provide us and the knowledge that was the object of his analyses are inescapably political. Foucault was, above all else, a political writer about knowledge.

And yet, should we follow this line of inquiry too far—that is, should we try to answer the question of what, in their essence, Foucault's writings *are*—we will only repeat the mistake against which his writings wage a ceaseless struggle. If Foucault was a political writer about our knowledge, it is not because he had anything to say about what our knowledge or our reason was like. Indeed, to speak of our knowledge or our reason (or even, at times, of our society) invites the kinds of blindness that have allowed our knowledges and the strategies within which they are engaged to continue their hold upon us. There is no Knowledge; there are knowledges. There is no Reason; there are rationalities. And so, just as it is meaningless to speak in the name of—or against—Reason, Truth, or Knowledge, so it is meaningless to engage in Politics. The idea that there is one true politics that will lead us to our salvation is a dangerous lie, as the Soviet experience will attest (Foucault 1976b, p. 459). Instead of Truth, there are truths; and instead of Politics, there is micropolitics.

The political aspect of Foucault's work has to be grasped through the concept of the micropolitical. Although there will be much to say about this later, a preliminary consideration of the micropolitical, and thus of the political, will offer an orientation that is useful for avoiding the misinterpretations that often accompany Foucault's poetic but labyrinthine texts. Foucault himself, when asked once for a definition of the political, offered this: "Every relation of force implies at each moment a relation of power (which is in a sense its momentary expression) and every power relation makes a reference, as its effect but also as its condition of possibility, to a political field of which it forms a part" (Foucault 1980a, p. 189). Politics he defined as "a more-or-less global strategy for co-ordinating and directing those relations." This definition points toward a conception of the political as an oriented field of power relations, relations wherein actions constrain and are constrained by other actions (Foucault, in Dreyfus and Rabinow 1982, p. 220), not in a haphazard fashion but rather in ways that possess their own logic and can be articulated.

Power is a network of interlocking constraints upon action (which is not to be equated with restraints upon action), rather than a force that one unitary class or body applies to another. It exists at many dispersed points, with more or less localized centers that themselves may or may not overlap or coordinate with one another. Thus it is possible to change or overthrow one set of power relationships without creating fundamental changes in other areas. The former Soviet Union provides a good example of this. Although private property was abolished, other power relationships remained in place, with the result that domination in Soviet society changed hands but was not fundamentally altered.

Such a picture of the political as a network rather than a hierarchy issues in a new picture of political understanding and political intervention. Instead of looking for the Archimedean point at which the fulcrum of power relationships can be altered, one must seek out the different types of power relationships that inhere in different areas. There is one type in psychiatry, another in medicine, yet another in sexuality: intersecting perhaps, but reducible neither to one another nor to a model that would explain them all. Power relationships are to be found on the micropolitical level, in the localities they invest rather than in a source from which they emerge.

This is not to deny any efficacy attaching to larger centers of power, for instance the state. The state is far from a political irrelevance. To recast the political in terms of the micropolitical is instead to acknowledge that the larger centers have too often been the focus of attention, resulting in a warped account of power and a vitiated conception of political intervention. Further, it is to recognize that, in order to exist, the power of institutions such as the state depend, at least in part, on smaller, more capillary relations of power. The local operation of power does not preclude its concentration at certain points, but it does serve as a reminder that the concentration of power should not be mistaken for its source. To refuse to see power at its points of heaviest concentration would be a blindness to the manifest; to refuse to see it anywhere else, however, is to be a slave to its manifestness.

Foucault's turn to the micropolitical is a unique event in twentieth-century social theory. It distinguishes him from many of his contemporaries with whom he has been compared, and even from those with whom he had the closest of personal ties. Certainly, the micropolitical is a movement away from traditional Marxism, for which there is, in essence, one class struggle with one analysis of one power relationship—that of the exploitative extraction of surplus value. However, there is also much distance here from the Critical Theorists, who, like Foucault, take the analysis of rationality to be a politically central task.

In the most famous of the Critical Theorists' texts, *Dialectic of Enlightenment*, Max Horkheimer and Theodor Adorno (1972, p. 4), in a vein that has been mistaken for that of Foucault, write: "Power and knowledge are synonymous." Knowledge, for Horkheimer and Adorno, is of one type. It is the calculable rationality bequeathed to us by the Enlightenment. Rationality has become an objectivity turned against the subject who uses it, who has in turn become an object among others: calculable, manipulable, reified. To be unknown means to be an as yet unreduced variable of an equation; and to be known means to have a solution within one. Here the dialectic is that between enlightenment and myth; as enlightenment moves farther away from the mythical whose task it was to escape, the closer it comes to a return to myth. Enlightenment itself, its mathematical formalism, is the new myth. Everything is explained by enlightenment rationality, and all that is asked of us is to conform to the rituals that structure it. Resistance is impossible, except within a silent realm untouched by a language that has itself become a prime agent bearing enlightenment values.

Although often accused of rejecting rationality (e.g., Habermas 1987, Dews 1987), Foucault never wrote a line after *Histoire de la folie* implying that the political problem of Western epistemology is reason. Seeing reason in connivance with domination presupposes a position that Foucault's work calls into question: that there is in our world an isolable phenomenon called "reason" which calls for our investigation. "I think that the word 'rationalisation' is a dangerous one. The main problem when people try to rationalise something is not to investigate whether or not they conform to principles of rationality, but to discover which kind of rationality they are using" (Foucault 1981, p. 226). Reason is a complex phenomenon—too varied, too disparate, and too concrete for the univocity of a single category. It can be neither rejected nor accepted wholesale, but only in part as it applies to specific situations that must themselves be analyzed.

Despite his friendship with Gilles Deleuze, and his sympathy for Deleuze's work with Felix Guattari (exemplified by his preface to *Anti-Oedipus* [Deleuze and Guattari 1977]), Foucault's own position is as far from theirs as from the Critical Theorists. While valuing their critique of psychological thinking and the Nietzschean ring of their positive conception of desire, he kept his distance from the naturalist foundations that a transcendental concept of desire requires. Joy is certainly to be found in difference, and the resistance Foucault often alluded to was nothing if not an affirmation of difference. But to found difference in a desire that is either unfettered or in a constant play of deterritorialization and reterritorialization requires the positing of an origin that Foucault explicitly rejected as early as *The Archaeology of Knowledge.*

Deleuze, like Nietzsche, longs for the purity of the wild state of things, and thus the object of his affirmation, like that of Horkheimer and Adorno, is on the other side of reason. And though Horkheimer and Adorno lament a world turned wholly against itself, while Deleuze celebrates the coming of an intruder that is nevertheless at home, they are agreed that oppressor and oppressed are a grander thing than Foucault would have found cause to admit. Foucault was too much the historian for origins and too much the micropolitician for grand strategies. His work found its roots in a world that owed more to the lowly than to the noble or the demonic; his analyses hinged more on the use and abuse of names than on the objects those names are intended to denote.

Herein also lies his difference from that other French social theorist with whom he has been identified, Jean-François Lyotard. Lyotard, the harbinger of the postmodern epoch, sees liberation, as did Foucault, in the proliferation of microstrategies. Like Foucault as well, he rejects the temptation of a naturalist, presocial origin. But, in a move that cuts across the grain of Foucauldian thought, Lyotard dedicates himself to thinking through the contemporary world from the perspective of a single principle: that of the breakdown of the grand narrative. What Lyotard wanted to study and to promote he called "paganism," the proliferation of partial, irreducible narratives (Lyotard and Thebaud 1985, p. 59). And so, for him, the emergence of micropolitics was more than the object of analysis; it was in itself the object of affirmation. There is, of course, a paradox here. One seeks partial narratives in the same way one used to seek grand narratives, without regard to the context or the network within which they become meaningful. This approach, however, leads directly back to traditional philosophy. Once micropolitics is no longer a perspective within which to perform investigation, but rather a strategy to be valued, then it too becomes a grand narrative, generating the same questions, doubts, and need for foundations that were once the province of the grand narrative preceding it.

For Foucault, the concept of micropolitics referred not to an object of valuation but to a perspective of investigation. Like Wittgenstein's notion of "language games," micropolitics is a picture of things. It is a picture that can be defended as such—one can, for instance, make the case that it is a more accurate picture than others—but not affirmed as a strategy for action. Within the picture, there may be much that is to be accepted or rejected; but that is because the picture shows these things to us. It is not the picture itself, then, that is useful in forming micropolitical strategies of resistance, but the things it reveals, the analyses it offers, and the conclusions that emerge from looking at the world by means of it.

The notion of the grand strategy, of Politics, whether in the form of critiques of Reason, of originary affirmations of desire, of paradoxical valuations of micropolitics itself, or of the traditional liberal or Marxist statist positions, is anathema to the work of Foucault. Instead of seeking to ground his analyses in any of these foundations, he sought to define a new form of intellectual work that would address particular strategies of oppression, offer particular historical and philosophical analyses, and, on occasion, recommend particular types of resistance. Regarding the last point, Foucault was particularly reticent, shunning, as Deleuze called it, "the indignity of speaking for others" (Foucault 1977b, p. 209). When it came to strategies for action, he preferred to listen to the oppressed rather than to act as the standard-bearer for their "liberation." Instead, he offered specific historical analyses that were useful for their struggle. The name he gave to one who performed this type of work was the "specific intellectual."

"Specific intellectuals" work "not in the modality of the 'universal,' the 'exemplary,' the 'just-and-true-for-all,' but within specific sectors, at the precise points where their own conditions of life or work situate them (housing, the hospital, the asylum, the laboratory, the university, family and sexual relations)" (Foucault 1980a, p. 126). Rather than standing above or outside their society, "specific intellectuals" are immersed within it. They cite, analyze, and engage in struggles not in the name of those who are oppressed, but alongside them, in solidarity with them, in part because others' oppression is often inseparable from their own. This type of intervention allows them to embrace the oppression that "universal intellectuals" used to analyze and to understand it better than the latter did, because rather than pronouncing on the fate of others from on high or outside, they carry with them an experience of the kind that belongs to the oppressed themselves. "Specific intellectuals" find that "they have often been confronted, albeit in a different form, by the same adversary as the proletariat, namely the multinational corporations, the judicial and police apparatuses, the property speculators, etc." (Foucault 1980a, p. 126). The particular interventions of these intellectuals do not exclude them from participating in the traditional struggles. The new focus does not mean that the old problems have all been resolved or have taken on a new form. Rather, the place of the intellectual within the old problems is being redefined. Now, instead of telling others about their oppression, instead of drawing from it its truth and its place in their lives, the task of intellectuals is to stand in solidarity with those whose situation forces them to struggle. This task confers upon the intellectual no privileged status. The intellectual has no more authority than the doctor or the lawyer to speak the truth or the meaning of others' struggles, and certainly no more than those who face their oppression daily. He or she is one of them in his or her own oppression, and beside them in theirs. It is a role of the walk-on, not of the director.

What the intellectual has lost in passing from universal overseer to specific participant is the garment of final arbiter in which one could once cloak oneself. It had been the task of the intellectual to give grounds, the final and true grounds, to which struggles appealed for justification and from which they proceeded toward action. (That this image often had little enough to do with reality was, of course, irrelevant to intellectuals. They found—and still find—themselves facing the choice of being either superfluous or dangerous to the struggles they engage in.) This place of final arbiter derived from the intellectual's—and particularly the philosopher's—claim upon the transcendental, the *a priori*, and the necessary: in short, upon the grounds from which truth and goodness emerge.

What Foucault is aiming at, both in his attempt to articulate the role of the "specific intellectual" and in his rejection of the forms of Politics engaged in by his contemporaries, is no less than a subversion of the very grounds from which philosophy has traditionally spoken. That his work is political, and in a new sense, we have already seen. We must see that it is also epistemological. In the very gesture by which he articulates a new form of political struggle and political self-understanding, he tries to shake the foundations of the entire philosophical edifice that gave sanctuary to the old forms—the transcendental forms—of political struggle. It is not merely a matter of raising another structure on the same grounds, but of ridding the grounds of the very possibility of supporting a foundation at all.

It is this that makes his abiding of grander political pronouncements next to his own micropolitical analyses so unsettling. When Foucault says "I do not mean in any way to minimise the importance and effectiveness of State power" (Foucault 1980a, p. 72), we want to disbelieve him. After all, don't his analyses of micropowers have the precise aim of supplanting the concept of an effective state? However, Foucault is not disingenuous here. His analyses are not intended to, and do not effectively, offer a substitute for traditional notions of power and their source in the state. They are instead analyses of other types of power relations, analyses that do not replace but complement the traditional analyses. And that is precisely why his work is so subversive.

When statist or other foundationalist political analyses are accepted alongside the micropolitical ones, doubt is cast upon the very idea that there is a source from which power originates, and thus a ground from which it can be derived. Were Foucault merely to say "Power is not this, it is that," he would not have carried his project beyond the ken of traditional political thought. There would have been arguments about what power really is, which would have relied on competing foundations of how things really are, and the radical implications of Foucault's micropolitical analyses would have been lost. It is precisely the moment of addition or supplementation (and not just a political supplementation but a historical one as well: micropolitical power is a recent phenomenon) that gives the radical edge to Foucault's thought. There is not just one form of power, there are many: many micropowers, many macropowers. And each, in order to see how it works and how it came about, requires its own specific interrogation.

For Foucault, the doublet he called power/knowledge is more than just an object of analysis. It is a definition of his project from the inside.

Many skeptical questions are bound to stalk a project of this nature and radicality. What reasons do we have to give up the traditional analyses in favor of micropolitical ones? What assurances are there that micropolitical analyses will lead to more than mere local reform? How will we decide between competing micropolitical analyses of the same situation? Such questions are important and worthy of address. However, they point to a deeper concern, one that haunts Foucault's work from beginning to end. It is a concern that, unaddressed, leaves one without the tools even to begin to formulate an answer to the foregoing questions.

Given that the project is not only political but epistemological as well, given that along with traditional political analyses Foucault's aim is to subvert foundationalist thinking itself, how is he ever to be able to justify his project? In what name, if not that of a truth or a justice he can defend against all comers, does he tell us to forget our foundations and to picture the world in micropolitical terms? Has Foucault not subverted the very possibility of grounding his project in the stroke by which he created it? As he admitted in *The Archaeology of Knowledge*, "my discourse, far from determining the locus in which it speaks, is avoiding the ground on which it could find support" (Foucault 1972a, p. 205). Was this avoidance ever rectified? And if not, what becomes of micropolitics? Why should his analyses move us, if he cannot even tell us why we should believe them?

From the archaeological works through the genealogical and ethical ones, the question of grounds shadows Foucault's writings. It is the constant complaint of his critics in the Frankfurt School (Habermas 1987, Dews 1987, Fraser 1981); and, for many, it was the string that unraveled the entire project. It is a question that must be confronted if Foucault's work is even to be found coherent, much less to be vindicated. The purpose of this study is to answer that question, to provide the epistemological grounds for Foucault's project.

Foucault's response to the question of grounds was always ambivalent. At times he seemed content with a historical relativism, saying that all truth—including his own—was relative to its historical situation. At others, he seemed to want to claim something more than a situated veracity for his works; but he never succeeded in articulating a measured and rigorous defense of that claim. What must be done, if the question of grounds is to receive an adequate response without betraying the diversity and often the dispersion on the basis of which it arises, is to grasp concretely how such a question can emerge in Foucault's writings, and then to see how—and whether—it can be answered.

The danger here is to see Foucault's writings as a uniform text that propounds a uniform theory which can be summed up and then questioned. We must reject the temptation of such an approach. Foucault's work is dispersed among the variety of his analyses; moreover, it is dispersed—and often within texts—among political, historical, ethical, and aesthetic concerns. John Rajchman saw Foucault's histories as doubly "nominalist": they were histories not of objects but of names and practices, and they were themselves perspectival (Rajchman 1985, pp. 50–52). His histories are also doubly dispersed: dispersed among the variety of political analyses he offers and also among those concerns which are political and those which are not. The risk in approaching Foucault's work for any sort of evaluation is that of obscuring or reducing these dispersions, without which his project is misapprehended.

In order to avoid such a mistake, we must follow a single theme of Foucault's works, to see the place it has within his histories and to articulate the question of grounds that emerges within it. That theme will be the critique of psychology, of psychological discourse and psychological practice.

The critique of psychology is a leitmotif in Foucault's texts. From his first major work through the last volumes of *The History of Sexuality*, he was preoccupied with the political and social implications of the practice and discourse of psychology. His earliest published works were, ironically, psychological texts (Foucault 1986b, 1976a). And later, when he waxed abusive, he was never so eloquent as when the object of his scorn was the practice of psychotherapists. This latter stance should not be astonishing, since the focus of much of his work was what he called "the genealogy of the modern subject" (Foucault 1980b, p. 3) and since he understood oppression to be linked to the ways in which people think about themselves.

While the critique of psychological discourse and practice (or, alternatively, psychological practice in its discursive and nondiscursive aspects) is a necessary component of the histories Foucault wrote, it is not, however, a central point about which his analyses revolve. The thread must not be mistaken for the whole fabric; moreover, as will be seen, the patterns woven from this thread change with changes in Foucault's own perspective. What was repression becomes creation; what was unitary becomes a multiplicity. In a sense, the thread that will be followed here is not so much one of a critique of psychological discourse and practice as of a series of critiques of psychological discourses and practices: an evolution and as well an overdetermination of the micropolitics of psychological events. The conceptions change with the contexts and with the development of Foucault's thought.

The motivation for such decentralized critique is both political and historical. Politically, it would be a betrayal of the movement of micropolitics to posit a principal type of power that would serve as the source—or even the model—of other power relationships. To do so would only substitute for statist or economistic theories of power another theory of sovereignty, and one that, inasmuch as it denied the political efficacy of points of concentrated power in favor of dispersion, would be more implausible than the theories it sought to replace. Historically, the emergence of psychology as a discipline is inseparable from an assemblage of events that have occurred over the past several hundred years, events that range over institutions as diverse as the clinic, the factory, and the prison, as well as the asylum. To view politics as an oriented field of multiple force relations is to view history as an intersection of multiple and irreducible events. Though some events and some intersections may be more important than others for some analyses, there is no place for a history that reduces all its phenomena to a single principle of explanation.

It will be objected as this study proceeds that, while preaching the necessity of taking Foucault's dispersive histories seriously, a preeminence has been granted to one period of his thought, the period of *Discipline and Punish* and the first volume of *The History of Sexuality*. After all, it was during this period that the concern with micropolitics emerged and the orientation to power relationships generally took precedence. Indeed, it will be asked, how can there even be a study of the type proposed here? If we are to avoid betraying the dispersion in Foucault's thought, should there not instead be a series of studies, perhaps even an infinity of studies, dealing with the grounds of his thought?

There is truth to this objection. Just as we have undertaken an attempt to ground Foucault's thought from a single perspective—that of micropolitics—and by recourse to the questions arising from a single avenue of investigation—that of the critique of psychology—other studies could inhabit other perspectives and take other avenues with no less of a claim for recognition than this one. A distinction that will be drawn as this study progresses is that between grounds and foundations, between offering justifications and excluding the possibility of doubt or debate. If this study offers grounds for Foucault's histories and his critiques, it does not offer a foundation. Other grounds could perhaps be drawn. In this respect, Foucault's texts are open ones.

This openness does not preclude all articulation, however. All texts, no matter how dispersed, could always be more so. If attention has been called here to the dispersive nature of Foucault's project, our purpose has not been to argue that there are no unities associated with his work. Unities abound even in the multiplicities of Foucault's studies—unities called madness, delinquency, and sexuality, to name a few. What unifies these things, however, is not their emergence from a foundation of truth that would cause them to be unsurpassable perspectives on their objects. Rather, it is that they give form to a historical multiplicity. It is a form that is arguably justifiable on the basis of historical record, politically useful for those engaged in struggle in our society, and, because these are histories of our own emergence, philosophically enlightening for those who seek an answer to the question: What is our present?

2

THE ARCHAEOLOGY
OF PSYCHOLOGY

There is a unity to Foucault's archaeological works. It appears, at first, to be a binary unity: that of the permitted and the forbidden, of the included and the excluded. There are the sane; and then there are the mad. There are the healthy; and then there are the sick. There are the discourses of knowledge; and there are the discourses without place. Either one is inside the comforting but conforming space of reason, health, and knowledge, or one is an outsider, condemned to the rituals of exclusion that one's society has constructed for the purpose of protecting—and monitoring—its own. That the rituals of exclusion *create* the distinction between inside and outside does not matter; however they may have arisen, the distinctions are there, and they are there to ensure obedience.

This picture is not entirely without resonance in the archaeological writings. It portrays accurately the project of social inscription that Foucault discovers in the emergence of the disciplines he investigates. However, there is an element missing in the binary schema; and the element this schema misses was, for Foucault, the crucial one, because it constituted the factor of resistance. The archaeological writings operated not on a binary system but on a ternary one: inclusion/exclusion/transgression. Transgression was the irreducible third element that, while refusing accommodation with the structure of inclusion, was unable to be banished from the territory which that structure enclosed. Nietzsche is a touchstone of Foucault's early—as of his later—thought. In the archaeological writings he appears as the mad philosopher, the insane transgressor. Later, when transgression gives way to resistance, he will reappear, this time as the patient—if still subversive—genealogist of *Discipline and Punish* and *The History of Sexuality*.

Transgression is the affirmation of difference. It is the joyous play of that which can neither be held captive by the gaze of the Same nor relegated by the Same to the darkness of the Other. Transgression speaks to the Same, but in a language whose phrases disturb without being wholly understood. Crossing and recrossing the limit between the included and the excluded, it is pursued by the forces of reason, health, and order, who seek either to appropriate it or to confine it. "Transgression, then, is not related to the limit as black to white, the prohibited to the lawful, the outside to the inside, or as the open area of a building to its enclosed spaces. Rather, their relationship takes the form of a spiral, which no simple infraction can exhaust" (Foucault 1977b, p. 35). And thus transgression is always at risk, always in danger of being either captured or exiled by the structure it seeks to disrupt.

Who, then, are the transgressors? Where do they come from, and what is the language—at once provocative and irrecuperable—they speak? They are not simply the mad, nor the sick. They are not those who merely refuse to speak in the words of the *epistēmē*. For them there are asylums, hospitals, and reform schools. The transgressors are the artists, those whose words and images are picked from familiar forms, but who twist and distort those forms in order to place before us a monster that is nevertheless born of our flesh and blood. They do this not to condemn us, for they, unlike us, are not subjects of the Same. Rather, they are seeking, and at times revealing, routes of escape from the monotonous repetition of domination and servitude that is the routine of daily life in the modern age. Artists are men and women in hegira who, since they cannot transcend the world they inhabit, choose instead to create figures and movements within it with which they are capable of living.

John Rajchman (1985), in writing about the place of the artist in Foucault's archaeological works, notes that in Foucault's thought modern art possesses three distinctive characteristics. First, modern art is about the essence of art itself. Second, the essence of art is the essence of all experience—or at least of contemporary experience. Last, modern art exists in a culture preoccupied with language and discourse. In such a context, it becomes the task of the artist to reveal to a culture those disruptive forces it has secreted away. But the task involves dangers. To plumb the depths of one's own historical experience is to lay aside the forms that orient one to the world around one. It is to cease abiding by the rules within which one has come to understand one's experience. The risk of transgression is the risk of exclusion, whether that exclusion be incoherence, sickness, or finally madness.

Thus, madness is both the source and the peril of art. As art defines the limit of culture and society with its constant play of transgression, so madness defines the limit of art. Madness is, in its resistance to the forces of inclusion, the place from which the artist begins the transgressive journey. It attracts him or her with a nearly irresistible force. Should one succumb to it, however, one is no longer an artist, but only a madman. In order to understand Foucault's early view of madness, it is necessary to see how madness interacts with what Foucault calls "reason" in his first major work.

In *Histoire de la folie* and its English abridgment, *Madness and Civilization*, the division between reason and madness that occurred between about 1650 and the late 1700s was a decisive one in the history of Western culture.[1] Referring to this division in a later interview, Foucault commented: "I was thinking of a whole series of binary oppositions which had each in its own way fed on the great opposition between reason and unreason that I had tried to re-constitute *à propos* of madness" (Foucault 1980a, p. 185). The division between reason and madness is that between the unconfined and the confined or, better, between two forms of confinement: the excluded and the included.

The act of social division was not a new one in Western culture. In fact, some of the institutions used in confining the mad were the leprosaria left over from the Middle Ages, institutions that had been awaiting "a new incarnation of disease, another grimace of terror, renewed rites of purification and exclusion" (Foucault 1965, p. 3). However, if the form of the act was not original, what it introduced into the social body was. Henceforth, there were to be two realms of discourse with absolutely no relation between them, neither epistemic, nor moral, nor even physical. The act of division between reason and madness, inaugurated by the confinements of the

---

1. Foucault's writings are not only philosophically but also historically controversial. For the purposes of this study, Foucault's own rendering of historical record will be accepted. However, that rendering has been questioned—with various degrees of comprehension of Foucault's project—by historians such as Rousseau (1972/73), Huppert (1974), Midelfort (1980), and Spierenberg (1984).

seventeenth century, was to set the course and define the parameters of thought and culture for at least the next three hundred years.

The Great Confinement which initiated this division was a decisive event. It constituted a break with the Renaissance that was total, both historically and epistemically, and even perhaps geographically (although on this last point Foucault is more reticent; see, for example, Foucault 1983a). Historically, the break was evidenced by the vigor with which confinement, previously practiced only sporadically, was pursued. Foucault points out that the first Hôpital Général was opened in 1656, and within a year one percent of the population of Paris was confined to one of the Parisian general hospitals. Although from a twentieth-century perspective the Great Confinement appears to have followed no clear principle, Foucault insists that nevertheless at the time there was one. "[W]hat is merely for us an undifferentiated sensibility must have been, for those living in the classical age, a clearly articulated perception" (Foucault 1965, p. 45). In fact, even if not clearly articulated, there was at least a diffuse moral and epistemic sensibility that informed the confinement, evidenced in the attitude expressed toward the mad by Descartes.

Descartes' *Meditations* was, according to Foucault, the philosophical expression of the exclusion of the mad from the discourse of reason. This exclusion was performed not in the name of truth; indeed, it is error that forms the basis for methodical doubt. Rather, it is in the name of the subject who doubts that madness is excluded. Madness precludes not only truth but error, because madness is the absence of the thought that permits both to exist: "madness is precisely the condition of impossibility of thought" (Foucault 1972b, p. 57; my translation). Thus madness is not merely error but the incapacity to become the subject of thought—and thus of truth or of error—at all.

Descartes' exclusion of the mad was in keeping with a broad sensibility infusing the mid-seventeenth century. In the several centuries before him, madness was seen not as an absence but instead as a figure whose presence was woven into the fundamental issues of human life. Madness revealed truth or death, it mocked men or punished them for their ways of error, it taunted reason without submitting to the taming that reason was later to impose on it. It was, in a word, transgressive. Renaissance madness, if not exactly art, performed within art—and perhaps at times within life—the transgressive function, a function that would later be the province of writers such as Sade, Artaud, and Bataille.

However, in the mid-seventeenth century all that was to end. Through a gradual process of exclusion, the mad were to be cut off from the social fabric and placed under the guardianship of a reason that would no longer tolerate the excesses that madness had once produced. The ascendance of reason, for Foucault a historical event,[2] was the reduction to silence of a madness that, if not wholly accepted, was at least free from the systematic procedures of exclusion that have characterized reason's dealings with it for the past three centuries.

But what then is this reason, whose emergence as a unified experience brought such changes in its wake? As Foucault points out, those who were sequestered during the Great Confinement were not only the mad but the poor, the indigent, and the inconvenient as well. The Great Confinement aimed at "a population without resources, without social moorings, a class rejected or rendered mobile by new economic developments" (Foucault 1965, p. 48). Clearly, the unity of the confinement that inaugurated the age of reason was not just the expression of outrage at irrational thinking, but was instead anchored at a deeper level in the culture in which it arose.

That Foucault intends by his use of the term "reason" more than just logical thinking is made clear in a passage describing "[t]he marvelous logic of the mad which seems to mock that of the logicians because it resembles it so exactly." In fact, "[t]he ultimate language of madness is that of reason, but the language of reason enveloped in the prestige of the image, limited to the locus of appearance which the image defines" (Foucault 1965, p. 95). The language of reason is a logical one, then, but reason itself is more than merely formal. It is also a relation to the content of language, to truth and morality.

Reason's relation to truth is defined negatively, since the very act that establishes reason's dominance is an act of excluding its Other. To have a proper relation to truth is to refrain from believing in false images; it is to understand the difference between what is illusory and what is real. The madman, in the classical age, is more than a dreamer. Reasonable people dream, too, but they do not take their dreams for reality. "Madness is precisely the point of contact between the oneiric and the erroneous" (Foucault 1965, p. 106). In madness, what is affected is the faculty of belief, which no longer withholds its assent from appearances which are only appearance but succumbs to a temptation to take appearance for reality.

2. Shoshana Felman (1975, p. 216) points out that the famous Foucault–Derrida debate hinges not so much upon what Descartes really said about the mad, but upon whether madness as the Other of reason is a historically instituted event or one that—as Derrida holds—is a permanent Other haunting all discourse.

Recall here the gesture by which Descartes dismissed the mad, "whose brain is so troubled and befogged by black vapors that they continually affirm that they are kings when they are paupers" (Descartes 1951, p. 18).

However, reason is more than a relation to truth. If it were not, we would still fail to understand why, in addition to the mad, the poor and the undesirable were also confined at the outset of reason's ascendance. In the classical age, there is a bond between reason and morality, just as there is a bond between reason and truth. It is a bond that finds its expression in the classical attitude toward work.

Confinement, instituted during a period of economic crisis, of high unemployment and low wages, required a labor on the part of many of its victims that continued until after the crisis was well over. Houses of confinement found themselves having to care not only for the indigent but also for those who were becoming indigent by the depression of wages that confined work produced. The labor of the confined was not, then, intro-duced simply to address the material needs of the early capitalist economy. Often, its effect was the opposite. There was a moral value to labor that, remunerated or not, economically efficient or not, was essential to the proper functioning of a reasonable being. "What appears to us today as a clumsy dialectic of production and prices then possessed its meaning in a certain ethical consciousness of labor, in which the difficulties of economic mechanisms lost their urgency in favor of an affirmation of value" (Foucault 1965, p. 55).

The institution of this affirmation of value was the responsibility of the state. Morality was becoming a public matter—an administrative matter—and, in contrast to the preceding centuries, it was the business of the state to see to the proper moral education of the individuals under its rule. Here, in contrast to Foucault's later views, individualizing power was ascribed largely to a mechanism operating at the state level. The induction into morality, which was to emerge as the primary form of treatment for the mad, was the business not of a thousand small and dispersed practical networks, but of the centralized and expanding administrative power that arose during the early capitalist period.

A picture of reason thus emerges which is the intersection of a relation to truth and a relation to morality. A person of reason was one who directed his energies toward productive labor and who did not take what was image for what was reality. In this picture, there was no place for the mad. The Renaissance role of jester of truth or mocker of death had no function in a society whose ethic was work and whose relation to truth was a straightforward one. Rather, the mad constituted, more than the poor or the indigent, the greatest threat to the sovereignty of reason:

> A culture like that of the Classical age, so many of whose values were invested in reason, had both the most and the least to lose in madness. The most because madness constituted the most immediate contradiction of all that justified it; the least because it disarmed madness entirely, leaving it quite powerless. This maximum and minimum of risk accepted by the Classical culture in madness is perfectly expressed in the word 'unreason': the simple, immediate reverse side of reason; and this empty, purely negative form, possessing neither content nor value, which bears the imprint of a reason which has just fled, but which remains for unreason the *raison d'être* of what it is. (Foucault 1972a, p. 192; translation from Sheridan 1980, p. 31)

Reason, then, dealt with the threat of madness by both pronouncing it to be nothing and, through confinement, reducing it to nothing. Madness became a silence about which reason spoke, ostensibly in a dialogue with it but really in a monologue upon it. But that was not all. As the classical age progressed, a new relation to madness took form, one that distinguished madness from other forms of unreason and gave it the place it occupies today. That new relation occurred in a space created by a change in the bond between morality and madness.

At first, this change was diffuse. The line between the ethical and the epistemic was not clearly drawn, allowing medical, philosophical, and moral interpretations to mingle indifferently in the interpretation of and intervention into madness. However, over the course of the seventeenth century, especially around hysteria and hypochondria, "a dynamics of corporeal space was replaced by a morality of sensibility" (Foucault 1965, p. 146). Hysteria began to appear as a disease which, if of the body, was nevertheless brought about by laxity (and which therefore affected women more than men). Soon after, it came to be understood as an affection entirely of the soul, arising through an excess of stimulation that was indicative of a sinful life. Instead of holding the cause of hysterical and hypochondriacal forms of madness to be deluded belief, the classical age came to see deluded belief as caused by an immoral existence. "What had been blindness would become unconsciousness, what had been error would become fault, and everything in madness that designated the paradoxical manifestation of non-being would become the natural punishment of a moral evil" (Foucault 1965, p. 158).

This change in perspective was complemented by a new interpretation of the techniques used in dealing with the mad. Measures such as purification through blood replacement and immersion in cold water started to take on new meanings. No longer were these interventions purely physical; now they were understood as rectifications of a moral fault as well as of an inadequately structured body and consciousness. What was needed was to cleanse an impure life rather than to cure a sick body. Consequently, the techniques of therapy, while remaining essentially unchanged, were reinterpreted. (Such a reinterpretation would occur again under the auspices of Samuel Tuke and Phillipe Pinel, who would use devices such as cold showers to punish a responsible being, rather than to cleanse or to cure it.)

Alongside this new interpretation of medical techniques arose a change in therapeutic goal from truthfulness to normality. Now, what was sought in the therapeutics of madness was no longer a restoration of the truth to one who had lost the capacity to recognize it, but a reintegration into society of one who had chosen to stray from the paths society had marked out.

These changes in interpretation and intervention, however, were occurring only in the private practice of doctors. They did not extend to the confines of the hospital. The purpose of the hospitals continued to be one of exclusion, of drawing the dividing line between reason and its Other. There was thus an ambivalence regarding madness in the classical age that was to be resolved only at the end of the eighteenth century. On the one hand, madness was to be exiled from the territory of reason, treated alongside the other failures of unreason such as poverty or sinfulness. On the other hand, madness was to be ascribed to deficiency, and reversed by procedures—at first primarily medical, then increasingly moral—designed to repair what nature or the individual had not sufficiently tended to. On the one hand, the state administered morality through exclusion; on the other, the doctor administered morality through reintegration. Two separate figures that, through the increasing moralization of madness, were bound to meet—and did, in the practices of Tuke and Pinel.

Tuke and Pinel ended the classical age treatment of the mad by establishing with finality that the moral responsibility of madness belonged to the mad person him- or herself. In opposite but complementary ways—Tuke through the use of religion, Pinel through a rejection of it—these "reformers" introduced methods of treatment and reinterpreted old methods of treatment whose effect was not so much to liberate the mad from their chains as to interiorize those chains within madness itself. Henceforth, madness was no longer an affliction to be borne; it was an inadequacy or immaturity to be overcome. The hospital, once a place of exile, was now to be a place of cure. But this cure was no longer physical. It was not to take place upon madness, but rather within it. Madness was to be treated by introducing into the asylum the same bourgeois relationships that were defining for the society outside it: family–child relationships, transgression–punishment relationships, madness–disorder relationships (Foucault 1965, p. 274).

The conceptual determination of madness initiated by Tuke and Pinel has endured up to our time. Rather than corroding the authority of reason, madness is now subject to it, physically by relegation to the asylum and morally by guilt in the face of itself. The psychiatrist and the psychologist are the voice of reason, while the mad are those forced to listen to their monologue. No matter that it is often the psychologist and the psychiatrist who are silent, while the mad speak; for if they speak, it is in the language of reason, with its inflections, and to the end of submitting to its regimen.

But if madness has been silenced, its force has found expression elsewhere: in Nietzsche, in Artaud, in the artists who, if not mad, construct a madness which is a disease within reason. It is true that madness precludes art; it is the point at which art no longer is. Yet there is an art that touches madness and gives expression to the forces of disorder inherent within it. For Foucault, this art, because it cannot be subdued, subverts the project of reason in a way that madness no longer can. "After Sade and Goya, and since them, unreason has belonged to whatever is decisive, for the modern world, in any work of art: that is, whatever any work of art contains that is murderous and constraining" (Foucault 1965, p. 285).

In *Histoire de la folie*, the critique of psychology is a critique of reason, of its domination and exclusion. Psychology emerges as the policeman and the guardian of reason, entrusted to keep madness at bay through a combination of exclusion and reintegration—or, better, exclusion in its physical and spiritual aspects. Armed with morality and cloaked in the mantel of truth, psychology discharges its duties with all the vigor that our society has been witness to since the time of Tuke and Pinel. It sunders from society a madness that disrupts by its very presence, and creates instead a tamer, more docile madness. Psychology, aligned with the powers of bourgeois society, has emerged as the primary spokesperson of the truth which is reason against the error which is transgression.

But if the discourse of reason is that of truth, how much truth will reason itself be able to stand? Reason is, after all, historical, existing not apart from the discourses that surround it but immersed within them. If it has defined itself through its exclusion of its Other, this is because it is not a ground to which history can always return, but instead a discourse subject to history itself. It is possible, then, to turn the investigation around, to determine the contours of reason not only by seeking what it excludes, but inversely by investigating its own landscape. This investigation Foucault called *Les Mots et les choses*, or in English *The Order of Things*. "The history of madness would be a history of the Other—of that which, for a given culture, is at once interior and foreign, therefore to be excluded (so as to exorcize the interior danger) but by being shut away (in order to reduce its otherness); whereas a history of the order imposed on things would be a history of the same" (Foucault 1970, p. xxiv).

To construct a history of the Same, however, is not merely to perform an inversion of a history of the Other. By the time of *The Order of Things*, a crucial assumption that underlay *Histoire de la folie* had been discarded: that of a transcendental force beneath history that helps give it form. That transcendental force in *Histoire de la folie* was not reason, of course, but madness; and its encrustation in a concrete history introduced an ambivalence into the notion of madness. On the one hand, madness is conceived of as a transhistorical transgression irreducible to the social order; on the other, it is the historically constituted object of reason that emerges over the course of the classical age. This ambivalence is gone by the time of Foucault's second book, *The Birth of the Clinic*. There he proposes to abandon "commentary," a hermeneutical procedure which assumes that an "unspoken element slumbers within speech, and that, by a superabundance proper to the signifier, one may, in questioning it, give voice to a content that was not explicitly signified" (Foucault 1973, p. xvi). *The Order of Things* continues this abandonment, analyzing discourses not in the negativity of what they suppress but in the positivity of what they create.

The Order of Things is not only more historical, but perhaps more limited in scope as well. In his preface to the English edition, Foucault (1970, p. x) wrote that he considered the book "not an analysis of Classicism in general, nor a search for a *Weltanschauung*, but a strictly 'regional' study." This limitation is at odds with the drift of many of Foucault's comments in the body of the work and was perhaps a product of such criticisms as Canguilhem's, which pointed out the inadequacy of assuming that the development of physics falls within a discontinuist model of epistemological change (Canguilhem 1967, p. 612). It also severely limits the concept of an *epistēmē*,

THE ARCHAEOLOGY OF PSYCHOLOGY   23

which presents itself as a general arrangement of knowledge within a given epoch. However, the acceptance of this limitation not only lends *The Order of Things* a greater historical plausibility, it also points the way toward the later genealogical works in its modesty.

As a discipline, psychology emerged later than the period covered in *Histoire de la folie*. That book left psychology at the threshold of its formation at the end of the classical age. In *The Order of Things*, psychology is seen to have a place not only in the repressive network of domination but in the network of knowledge as well. Its place in that latter network is determined not so much by its relationships with the social institutions in which it arises, but by the other knowledges with which it is connected by means of the *epistēmē* it inhabits.

An *epistēmē*, for Foucault, is the "conditions of possibility" (Foucault 1970, p. xxii) for empirical sciences at a given time. Those conditions are not transcendental, but historical; and they are not political or institutional, but epistemological and discursive. The conditions of possibility for a set of empirical sciences are the network or the "space" (p. xxii) within which those sciences are able to appear. The concept of an *epistēmē* implies that what is able to be said at a certain time (within the sciences) is not independent from other things that are able to be said; there is a regularity among regions of discourse such that a science, in order to be accepted as a science, must either mimic that regularity or complement it. The knowledge of a given period (or at least some regions of knowledge, given the above limitation), then, forms a whole whose conditions lie not outside it but within it: at the purely discursive level. An *epistēmē* is the "positive unconscious" (p. xi) of knowledge, giving rise to its forms without itself becoming transparent in them.

Thus, an *epistēmē* is not ideological. Its conditions do not lie within a set of nondiscursive practices of which it is merely the expression. Nor is it merely descriptive. It is a "historical *a priori*" which "delimits in the totality of experience a field of knowledge, defines the mode of being of the objects that appear in that field, provides man's everyday perception with theoretical powers, and defines the conditions in which he can sustain a discourse about things that is recognized to be true" (Foucault 1970, pp. 157–58).

The postclassical *epistēmē*, in which psychology took root (and the end of which we are currently witnessing), is characterized by an endless self-reflective mechanism within knowledge that continually drives it back upon itself. This self-reflective mechanism arose in the wake of the dissolution of classical representation, in which it was thought that knowledge presented itself clearly and distinctly through the transparent medium of language. Now, the medium of knowledge appears to be more opaque. In order to know, it is not enough to allow language to reveal the nature of things; one must grasp the knower as well as the known. It is only by coming to understand man, the being who knows, that knowledge will be able to touch upon the things themselves. With the end of the direct access of knowledge to things, all routes to truth lead through man. Man, and with him epistemology, are born contemporaneously.

The parameters of this postclassical *epistēmē* are fourfold (as they are for the other *epistēmēi* Foucault analyzes). First, there is an analytic of finitude, a turning of finitude upon itself in order to determine its own conditions. Man, who is finite, must investigate that finitude in order to understand its structure. Thus, second, man is an "empirico-transcendental doublet" (Foucault 1970, p. 318), the ground of knowledge and its object—and, more profoundly, the ground as object and the object as ground. Man is thought to be transcendental inasmuch as he is the object of an empirical investigation into the foundation of knowledge; and he is empirical inasmuch as he is investigated in order to discover the transcendental conditions he offers to knowledge. Third, there is the *cogito* and the unthought, the attempt by the *cogito* to grasp the source of its own activity in an ever-deepening helical movement that must, each time it discovers a source, seek the source of that source because the discovered source is already *cogito*. If I can think it, it must no longer be the source of my being able to think. Last, there is the retreat and return of origin, an endless search for the ever-receding origin of man's thought and activity, an origin that is always there because always founding, but never accessible because always beyond the thought that attempts to grasp it.

This is the complex of knowledge in the nineteenth century within which the science of psychology is born. Psychology, along with the other two human sciences of sociology and the analysis of literature and myth, occupies "the distance that separates (though not without connecting them) biology, economics, and philology from that which gives them possibility in the very being of man" (Foucault 1970, p. 353). Psychology, like the other human sciences, attempts to bridge the gap that separates man as a transcendental condition from man as an empirical objectivity. It is at the heart of the postclassical *epistēmē*, because it is the attempt to resolve the aporia that the postclassical *epistēmē* has opened up.

This attempted resolution, however, does not occur with a new set of terms, but with terms and methods borrowed from the already constituted sciences of biology, economics, and philology. In the case of psychology, the debt is particularly to biological science, whose analyses in terms of function and norm become the methodological bedrock upon which psychology erects its project. It has already been seen that the increasing moralization of the treatment of madness resulted in a change of values from which madness was to be accused, the change from truth to norm. Here a further refinement is introduced. At its inception, psychology views man primarily in terms of function, in terms of how it is that man operates. Thus, there can be several psychologies: one for the "average" person, one for hysterics, one for the dull-witted, and so on. As it progresses, however, psychology moves from this more dispersed orientation toward function to one based upon norms, in which the normal forms the pole around which the various abnormalities find their place. Dispersion gives way to totalization, and a unitary science of human behaviors and their deviations emerges.

At the same time, there is a movement not only within psychology but within the human sciences generally, so that psychology's prominence as a science of man is replaced, first by sociology and then by the analysis of literature and myth. These replacements do not mean, however, that the structure of subjectivity becomes less important. The analysis of literature and myth occurs in terms of signification and system, so that the demise of traditional psychology is followed by the ascendance of psychoanalytic theory and the related theories of the unconscious and its signifying activity. Psychology does not so much lose its significance as change its form and its methods, focusing less upon the behavioral constants of man and more upon his interiority.

The goal of psychology never varies, though. It is to discover the knower, to turn man into a transparency so that not only empirical humans but the transcendental ground of knowledge itself will become knowable. The pristine moment of the classical age when everything was accessible to those who desired to know will be recovered—or at least re-created—in the language of the postclassical *epistēmē*. The goal of psychological science is to render subjectivity, that subjectivity which is the subject of knowledge, objectively comprehensible: but as subject, not as object.

Psychology, then, like sociology and the analysis of literature and myth, is, for Foucault, the impossible project *par excellence* of the postclassical *epistēmē*. It is dedicated to rendering intelligible that which must necessarily escape all intelligibility. Man cannot be made transparent. The reason for this is not that human beings are of such depth and complexity that they cannot be understood in any exhaustive sense. Rather, it is the epistemic structure of psychology that bars the psychological project from its realization. At the core of this *epistēmē* lies a transcendental aporia which the psychological project cannot overcome. It is transcendental because it is the condition of all projects of knowledge; it forms the parameters within which all knowledge must occur. It is an aporia because it attempts to turn conditions of knowledge into an object of knowledge, thus setting in motion a self-reflective mechanism that is eternal, since it is unrealizable. "It is therefore not man's irreducibility, what is designated as his invincible transcendence, nor even his excessively great complexity, that prevents him from becoming an object of science. Western culture has constituted, under the name of man, a being who, by one and the same interplay of reasons, must be a positive domain of *knowledge* and cannot be an object of *science*" (Foucault 1970, pp. 366–67).

Thus, psychology is part of the central scaffolding of what Foucault (1970, p. 340) has called "the anthropological sleep." This sleep, which followed the dogmatic sleep of classical representation, is the slumber of an age content not to go beyond its anthropological models for answers to the questions that most deeply disturb it. Assuming that those answers are nowhere else but farther along the path it has trodden for a hundred and fifty years, the postclassical age turns toward the disciplines of psychology, sociology, and the analysis of literature and myth to provide the age, at the end of their inquiry, with the epistemological foundations it seeks.

It should not be surprising, then, that the figure that disrupts this sleep, the nonman who transgresses the territory of the postclassical *epistēmē*, is none other than the figure of madness itself. At the limits of psychoanalysis, where the postclassical age finds the themes preoccupying it—death, desire, and law—pushed to the edge of articulation, lies the mad nonbeing which subtends man. Madness is the nothingness upon which is founded the empirico-transcendental doublet, the nonorigin upon which the anthropological sleep rests. Our age, now at its most extreme point of development, which is also its point of dissolution, "sees welling up that which is, perilously, nearest to us—as if, suddenly, the very hollowness of our existence is outlined in relief; the finitude upon the basis of which we are, and think, and know, is suddenly there before us: an existence at once real and impossible, thought that we cannot think, an object for our knowledge that always eludes it" (Foucault 1970, p. 375).

Madness, as transgression and as art (once again the names of Nietzsche, Artaud, and Mallarmé are invoked), comes to haunt the postclassical *epistēmē* as it did reason in the *Histoire de la folie.* Art, as a mad void, an insane contingency, seeps into the depths of our transcendental aporia and pours poison on the site we had hoped to be our healing. A mad art or an artful madness, now not in the form of a positive force but instead as the most absolute contingency and arbitrariness, drifts to the surface of the dream-world that is the anthropological sleep and frightens it into a wakefulness that is the dissolution of our *epistēmē*. It is once again transgression, neither inside nor outside, but an outside that is coiled in the heart of the inside, that announces the fragility of an epistemic domination and betrays the weakness that will bring it down.

Histoire de la folie and *The Order of Things* present different, though not incompatible, images of psychological discourse and practice. Both of these images, the repressive collusion with reason and the transcendental aporia of man, are discovered through a method that Foucault called "archaeology." He lays out that methodology (with certain revisions) in *The Archaeology of Knowledge*. In order to understand the critique of psychology, it is necessary to grasp the archaeological method and to see whether the archaeology of psychology is a coherent approach to the study of the place of psychological thinking and practice in our culture.

Archaeologically, the discipline of psychology is treated without regard to the truth of the claims it makes. Shown neither as a progressive history nor as a retreat from a primitive intuition, psychology's hold upon the truth, whatever it may be, is irrelevant for one who would like to know the place of psychology in Western culture. This bracketing of truth is a radical one; it subverts the assumption that a discourse's being true provides a sufficient justification for its existence. Subversion, however, is not a denial of the value of truth. Foucault nowhere argues that there is no value to a discourse or discipline being true. Instead, he shows that there are effects which discourses have regardless of their being true or false, so that the truth of a discourse is no longer a sufficient defense for it to claim in the face of criticism. The emergence of a discourse is treated as an "event" (Foucault 1972a, p. 27), something to be investigated not in the depths of its truth or of its reference, but in the horizontality of its relations with surrounding discourses and practices.

Archaeology is not, however, a method of pure description. It is not merely a recitation of the practices of psychology and the discourse of those practices; it is an uncovering of the conditions that give rise to those practices and discourses. Although Foucault called those conditions "conditions of possibility" in *The Order of Things*, in *The Archaeology of Knowledge* he called them, more accurately, "conditions of reality" (Foucault 1972a, p.

127). Conditions of possibility, in the Kantian tradition, are those conditions which circumscribe the validity of certain discourses. They are the conditions that determine whether a discourse can be considered to be true. What archaeology is after is different; its project is not so much epistemic as historical. Given that a certain discourse did emerge, archaeology wants to discover what place it took up in the system of knowledge and practices that were current at the time and what use it served so that it and no other discourse emerged at that place and time.

The distinction Foucault makes in order to realize this difference between conditions of possibility and conditions of reality is one that lies within the French language, between *savoir* and *connaissance*. Although both words are usually translated as "knowledge," Foucault gives them each a technical meaning. "By *connaissance* I mean the relation of the subject to the object and the formal rules that govern it. *Savoir* refers to the conditions that are necessary in a particular period for this or that type of object to be given to *connaissance* and for this or that enunciation to be formulated" (translator's reference in Foucault 1972a, p. 15; original source not given). A *connaissance* is a specific discipline; psychology, for instance, is a *connaissance*. *Savoir*, on the other hand, is the set of conditions—epistemic or otherwise— without which it would be impossible for a specific discipline or *connaissance* to appear. These conditions are not transcendental but historical. They obtain during a given period and form the parameters within which all specific types of knowledge—or at least all types of knowledge within the domain of that *savoir*—appear. That these conditions are historical and not transcendental means that their validity-conditions, their conditions of possibility, are irrelevant for archaeological investigation. The conditions that determine whether a discourse can emerge have nothing to do with the progress of truth, but with factors that, if epistemic, are so only in a historically relative sense.

This latter implication is crucial. Foucault (1972a, pp. 114–15) points out that archaeology is a model and not a theory—that is, it is a perspective for understanding events and not a claim concerning how events really come about. If the archaeological model is to have any credence, however, it must at least deny that the emergence of discourses of truth can be reduced solely to the progressive unfolding of a correspondence between our theories about things and the way things really are. The *savoir/connaissance* distinction implies that there is an efficacy possessed by historical conditions in relation to the claims of knowledge made by different disciplines at different times.

What archaeology seeks to discover are "rules of formation" (Foucault

1972a, p. 74), rules that dictate what elements and what structures a discourse must possess in order to be admitted into the arena of knowledge during a given historical epoch. These rules are not chance regularities that are able to be seen in groups of discourses in various periods, but regularities that govern those discourses, although they inhere in the discursive practices themselves. The archaeology of psychology, then, seeks to situate psychological discourse and practice within the set of historical conditions that were at once necessary for its emergence and yet within the network of which it formed a thread. The questions that such an archaeology would answer are the following: What were the conditions of knowledge such that psychological discourse could take hold? What is the relation of psychological discourse to other discourses around it? Why did psychology and not another discourse arise in the time and the place in which psychology arose? In order to answer these questions, first the network of discourses that psychology inhabits is described. Then, the *savoir* or *epistēmē* governing this network is delineated. Finally, the relations between psychological discourse and other forms of practice are drawn.

This is exactly what is done in *The Order of Things*, a work that is both theoretically coherent and methodologically rigorous. But doing it involves three assumptions, each of which is open to question. First, there is an assumption that the regularities that archaeology notes in its descriptive phase refer to rules or laws that govern such regularities. This first assumption is related to a second one: that the discursive level, the level of what is said, can be separated from the nondiscursive level in the analysis of the rules of formation of discourses. Last, there is the assumption that all discourses have historical conditions that are, at least in part, determinative for what they are able to say. To cast doubt upon these assumptions is to question the viability of archaeology as Foucault conceives it; and, given the analytics of psychology he offers in his first two books, these assumptions are indeed open to such doubt.

The second assumption is the most generally questioned one. Deleuze (1988) points out that if the discursive and the nondiscursive are heteronomous, Foucault must offer an account of how they can also be related, which he does not do until his later works. The Althusserian Marxist Dominique Lecourt (1975) makes the charge that any assumption of the autonomy of the discursive ignores the material conditions in which it is embedded. But perhaps the most serious questions are raised by one of Foucault's own texts, *Histoire de la folie*. Was it not the very convergence of doctors' discourses on madness and the nondiscursive practice of confinement that created the conditions for psychological discourse as it is currently structured? Is not the problem of psychiatric repression—or, as Foucault will later call it, "psychiatric oppression"—the problem of a discourse that finds its roots in practices of domination that are partially discursive but also partially administrative and institutional? The separation of the discursive and the nondiscursive, even if only for purposes of analysis (Foucault 1972a, pp. 45–46), is a disengagement not justified by the historical record Foucault has put before us.[3]

The first assumption begs a series of Wittgensteinian questions about rules that have been offered by Hans Sluga (1985, p. 410). How are rules of discourse hidden, if indeed they are hidden? What is the causal efficacy behind a rule? Don't rules require examples in order to be followed? In short, isn't there something about a rule that distinguishes it from a mere regularity, some force or power that needs to be explicated before the citation of a regularity can be ascribed to a rule? The problem is this: Foucault's archaeological method moves from a description of regularities to an ascription of rules without offering any justification for the inference. To say that psychological discourse participates in an aporia in postclassical thinking is one thing; but to say that its statements are governed by that participation is something that requires a further defense, one that Foucault has not offered.

Moreover, Foucault seems precluded from offering such a defense. In sketching the space in which the archaeological method functions, he refuses to accept the traditional historical unities of continuity, influence, genre, and especially origin (Foucault 1972a, pp. 21–25). Without such a refusal, the archaeological project risks falling into the traditional historiological commitment to a comprehensive theory that will reduce historical divergences to a single matrix, thus betraying the unique space of change and difference it saw itself as tracing.

The third assumption is a relativist one. It is the generalization of the archaeological method as a model for all discursive formations, including our own. Foucault (1972a, p. 130) writes that "it is not possible for us to describe our own archive [an archive is the general system of discursive formations at a given time], since it is from within these rules that we speak." But if we cannot describe it, how do we know it exists (cf. Hoy 1979)? Historical relativism of the kind Foucault advocates in his archaeological writings is an incoherent thesis. To show how specific historical conditions

---

3. Further evidence against this assumption is supplied by the histories offered in *Discipline and Punish* and the volumes on the history of sexuality.

affected specific types of knowledge is certainly a tenable project; Foucault's historical work may have accomplished this. But to turn the specific claim into a general one about all knowledge is self-refuting: it denies to the claimant the ability to justify the claim.[4]

The criticism of these three founding assumptions of Foucault's archaeological method points to a problem that plagues the early writing: the return of the transcendental. Although Foucault dedicates himself to a radical historicization of principles that are normally considered to be atemporal foundations of thought, founding principles keep returning to haunt his own work. From beginning to end, Foucault's writings have as one of their central purposes to show how concepts, principles, assumptions, and methods that we take for granted as the givens of all thought are themselves subject to a history that can be described. And yet, such concepts, principles, assumptions, and methods find their way back into the very attempt at their subversion. Instead of the discursive being either epiphenomenal to practice or a progressive history of truth, it forms a closed unity with its own principles; instead of rules guiding discourse from without, there are rules guiding it from within; instead of a transcendental absolutism, there is an equally transcendental historical relativism.

Derrida (1978) asked of *Histoire de la folie* how it could purport to describe the silencing of madness by reason without repeating the crime of that silencing, since all talk must occur within the constraints reason has constructed. David Carroll (1978) posed a similar question to *The Order of Things*: How could the concept of an *epistēmē* remove us from the idea of a founding subject, when it took all the functions of foundation upon itself? These critics, and others like them, point to an aporia in Foucault's own thinking during his archaeological writings, an aporia that, like the return of the repressed, reemerges at the precise point where its exclusion is supposed to occur. It seems as though, in Foucault's early works, the act of subverting transcendental motifs—the founding subject, the *a priori*, the necessary—

---

4. Gary Gutting (1989, p. 273) has disputed the claim that Foucault's archaeologies are generally relativist: "His historical critiques of reason are always directed toward very specific applications (psychiatry, clinical medicine, the human sciences), with no suggestion that the inadequacies of any one domain can be extrapolated to others." However, concepts like "*epistēmē*" and "historical *a priori*," invoked by Foucault during his archaeological period to explain his terrain, do not readily lend themselves to such an interpretation; nor does Foucault's acknowledged break between his archaeological period and his genealogical one. What Gutting offers, it seems, is a reconstructive view—and, as such, a valuable one—of how the archaeological period ought to be read, given the perspective introduced by the genealogical turn. As such, Gutting's work is less successful as an interpretation than as a corrective.

occurs in a way that in fact allows a continuation of them. If, as Foucault (1988, p. 11) said in an interview in 1982, "All my analyses are against the idea of universal necessities in human existence," why do universal necessities—rules, self-enclosure, relativism, founding subjects—keep recurring in the attempt to eliminate them?

Foucault, it seems, was still looking for a principle with which to struggle against the principles considered to be founding for human thought. Unfortunately, to seek such a principle is to repeat the problem in a less coherent form. Madness, which—like art—is supposed to transgress the conceit of a self-satisfied reason, instead mirrors the assurances of a transcendental subject that reason gives itself. Indeed, even to invoke a unity such as reason is to invite a conception of self-enclosed practice that subverts the project of fracturing transcendental thought. Similarly, removing the powers of the subject to determine the parameters of thought, only to install those parameters in a set of anonymous rules of discourse, serves merely to displace the concept of foundations of thought, not to destroy it. To consider discourse as carrying its own historical principles is not to save its specificities from the ravages of either progressivism or materialism; it is only to ravage them in a new form, by quarantine rather than by exposure. To offer relativism as the answer to absolutism is to replace with one hand what is being removed by the other; absolutism does not die this way, it is only forced to lead a more shadowy existence.

The archaeological writings offered a critique of psychology, both political and epistemic, that opened out onto larger questions that its conceptual framework raised but was unable to answer. It is not that there was nothing right about what the archaeologist was trying to say about psychology. Indeed, many trenchant points were raised that remain untouched by the larger questions surrounding archaeology—the place of confinement, the moralization of madness, the derivative nature of psychological science and the aporia that stalks it. But how will we be able to conceive of these points, which ask us to reconsider our relationship to important areas in our own culture and thought, if the very attempt to think them through is merely a repetition of the same cultural and epistemic axes we are asked to put in question? How can we conceive of a historical study of psychology that avoids the twin traps of naive acceptance and self-defeating relativism? How can we conceive of a critique of psychology, and of the foundationalism to which it is bound, without reenacting the tired unities of subject, law, and necessity that gave rise to the need for critique? And, finally, how can we conceive of a resistance to psychology and to foundationalism that resides not just in madness or aesthetics but everywhere these forces of domination encrust themselves onto our daily lives?

3

THE GENEALOGICAL TURN

The events of May 1968 changed the landscape of French intellectual life. Although there was no transfer of power, although the universities later went into retrenchment and the traditional political organizations recovered their hegemony, although France now appears to be little changed from the time before the events, what occurred in 1968 had revolutionary effects upon the way power, politics, and resistance have come to be conceived. These effects were felt not only by the Parisian Left, but by those in other countries who either followed the events of May and their aftermath or who experienced their own events of May in their own countries: the Prague Spring or the Vietnam war protests in the United States. Suddenly, the old categories of political understanding were rendered obsolete, and new categories—as well as new forms of action—were being discovered and enacted.

The first casualty of the events of May was Marxism. Not that Marx's name was banished from leftist discourse; his concepts and his writings remained as vital a source of debate as ever. However, the political legacy that had derived from his work, and that in France went by the name of the Parti Communiste Français, lost completely and forever its claim to vanguard status on the left. Two events caused this loss. The first was the collusion of the Communists with the government in trying to quell the unrest. But, more important, people came to recognize that not only workers' parties but those suffering oppression of various kinds, whether organized or not, could rise up in their own name and with their own demands. Revolutionary changes were not the product of one struggle, during one stage of industrial development, led by one party, and ending in one form of society. Oppression, it was learned, was everywhere; everywhere it took on different forms; and everywhere it could be fought in separate, if intersecting, struggles.

Foucault was in Tunisia during the events of May (Sheridan 1980), but their effects were not lost on him, nor on those who had read his books. *Histoire de la folie, The Birth of the Clinic,* and *The Order of Things* were perceived to be, and indeed were, documents that recorded types of domination that could not be reduced to the traditional concept of the class struggle. When Foucault returned to France, first to head the philosophy department at the *gauchiste* Vincennes campus, then, in 1970, to take a chair at the Collège de France, he sought to understand the implications of this revolution without a center and to articulate a political position that would be commensurate with what it had revealed.

His first attempt was at his inaugural lecture at the Collège de France (in Foucault 1972a, pp. 215–37). It was a beautifully crafted analysis and a moving piece of oratory; its conclusions, though, were soon to undergo a major transformation. In this lecture, Foucault points out that discourse of all types is subject to the exclusions of power. These exclusions function in several ways: through prohibition, through division and rejection, but most insidiously through the distinction between the true and the false. It is not that truth is itself violent; but the will to truth, supported by a multitude of institutions and traditions, works to suppress the flourishing of discourses by subjecting them to a variety of constraints. Among these constraints are the unities that organize discourse in order to prevent the irruption of chance, of the irregular, or of the disorganized and the disorganizing—unities such as the founding subject, originating experience, and universal mediation.

The task of those who would free discourse from the constraints of power, then, is to find forms of articulation that disrupt the principles of the will to truth and restore to discourse its character as a material, irreducible event. Strategies for disruption include reversal, discontinuities, an emphasis on the specific rather than the universal, and a focus on the relations discourse has with that which is outside it rather than on its interior unity. Announcing his own future work, Foucault divides his subsequent analyses into two classes: the critical, whose goal is to discover forms of exclusion, and the genealogical, directed toward tracing the emergence of various discourses. Both types of analyses, however, converge in taking the third form of exclusion, that of the true and the false, as their object.

The inaugural lecture retains themes from Foucault's earlier archaeological period: the emphasis on power as a prohibitive force, binary and ternary oppositions, a focus on the discursive at the expense of the nondiscursive. However, it also announces a theme that, although it infused the earlier writings, was hereafter to become the centerpiece around which Foucault's histories would find their place. This new theme is the intertwining, the chiasm, of knowledge and power. Regarding the latter concept, though, Foucault was soon to perform a 180-degree turn, from considering it to be a negative and prohibitive force to treating it as a positive and creative one. This turn would remove him permanently both from traditional political analyses and from his own earlier histories (cf. Foucault 1980a, p. 184).

Both in liberal and in Marxist analyses, power is conceived as an essentially negative phenomenon. For liberal analyses (e.g., Hobbes 1968, Locke 1980, Mill 1978), power is the province of the state. The state defines the parameters of acceptable individual and institutional behavior (albeit with consensual or democratic permission) by exercising the power of prohibition upon all behaviors that are unacceptable to the community. The mechanism for such prohibition is the law, which in turn provides the model for the liberal conception of power. Within the space defined by law's parameters, the concept of power assumes less urgency. That space is defined as the space of freedom, the space open to individual and institutional choice of action. That some institutional or individual choices may constrain others is not, of course, irrelevant; it is, however, conceived on the model of state power—as a limitation of free action—and is to be dealt with through the mechanism of state power (i.e., law).

The Marxist concept of power is, if more nuanced, still of a piece with the liberal concept. Power, for the Marxist, is the exercise of repression by the state and economic apparatuses in order to ensure that capitalist exploitation of surplus value can take place efficiently. Exploitation itself is not power. Exploitation is an economic category, not a political one, which refers to the surplus value that is retained by the capitalist at the end of the working day (Marx 1976). Power, on the other hand, is the bourgeoisie's ability to ensure that exploitation will be able to take place. The characteristic means of doing this are, in traditional Marxism, violence and ideology (Poulantzas 1978). The project for the working class, consequently, is to arrogate to itself the power that forces it to suffer exploitation—a power that lies principally in the state—so that exploitation can no longer be effectively exercised and workers can retain what they produce. Thus, the two great strategies of the communist program: seizure of the state apparatus and worker ownership of the means of production.

What liberals and Marxists share, although their goals are diametrically opposed, is a conception of power that is negative or restrictive upon a subjectivity that would otherwise act in violation of the limits or coercions it marks out. Because power is prohibitive, and because the force it restricts is the potent field of a recalcitrant subjectivity, the seat of power must lie in a strong organization or institution. This is why the state figures so prominently in both analyses (although, for the Marxist, the need for a state should eventually decline as social relationships are gradually rearranged). Moreover, these negative conceptions of power have implications for how other concepts in the social field will be articulated, especially knowledge. For the liberal, knowledge occurs in the free space of subjectivity; it is, at least in its formation, not subject to the constraints of power. Indeed, the very definition of the traditional conception of knowledge—as a reflection of how things are—precludes knowledge from being a political event. Knowledge, as such, is alien to power. If it is appropriated or politicized, it is always after the fact, after it has become knowledge.

For the Marxist, knowledge is of two kinds. Either it is in accordance with the dialectical understanding of history, in which case it is both scientific and true; or it is ideology, an epiphenomenal expression of the relation of material forces in a given economic arrangement (cf. Althusser and Balibar 1970). Ideology is useless, except to the ruling class, for whom it is able to provide a smoke screen to cover its attempt to exploit those the ruling class employs. Dialectics, on the other hand, is more useful in the long run, because it reveals the movement of history and thus allows the exploited class to recognize and appropriate historical forces in its attempt to liberate itself. Unlike the liberal, the Marxist understands that knowledge is political; it is, however, inserted into a grid that identifies truth with liberation and falsity with subjection, thereby mirroring the liberal valorization of truth and precluding a political critique of truth. For the Marxist, as for the liberal, truth is good. It is falsity that must be eliminated.

Foucault's own view of the relation between knowledge and power, in the several years after the events of May, takes on a complexity possessed by neither of these two models, nor by his earlier writings. Like the Marxists, he came to believe that that relation is historical, and that knowledge is not removed from power. This, however, does not imply that a broad schema exists within which the relation can be charted, nor that truth can be valorized just because it is true. Knowledge–power relationships are multiple, existing not only in different forms at different times, but also in different forms at the same time. In order to understand them, one needs to investigate specific regions in which either knowledge is claimed or power is exercised; grids of comprehension, if they do exist, must emerge in the course of specific investigation rather than in an *a priori* reflection on the status of knowledge or of history in a given period.[1]

Moreover, power must be conceived not in terms of what it denies, represses, rejects, or excludes but rather in terms of what it creates. Instead of assuming that there is an object beneath power to which power applies its force, an object that has its own characteristics which it is trying to realize, Foucault began to consider power as creating its objects, as producing the very characteristics that traditional analyses hold up against power. Thus, subjectivity, conceived of by liberals and Marxists alike as the counterpoint to power, becomes in Foucault's view an effect of power. But here we must be cautious. It is not subjectivity *per se* that is an effect of power; indeed, the question can be asked whether there is such a thing as subjectivity *per se*. Rather, specific forms of subjectivity are effects of specific ways in which power is exercised; and it is always in the name of a specific subjectivity that those who would and those who would not change things speak. In the last period of his work, Foucault recounts the history of different forms of subjectivity and their relation to different exercises of power.

What are the implications of this revised view of knowledge, power, and their relationship for the study of psychology?

What is needed for an adequate grasp of the place of psychology in the social and political field is not an analysis of how psychological knowledge is used after it is gained, nor how it is related to the current state of production, but a tracing of its emergence as a discrete field of knowledge—its multiple sources, its various relationships, its heterogeneous effects. To perform a political study of psychological knowledge and psychological practice, it is necessary to view the psychological as a pattern in a larger cloth of practices and events, a pattern whose threads come from and return to different areas of the fabric and whose relation to other patterns is one of various degrees of similarity and difference—but not of expression and only at times of causality.

1. For more detailed analyses of the relation between Foucault and the Marxist tradition, see Poster 1984 and especially Smart 1983. See also Foucault 1980a, p. 118.

This is not to say that there are no greater patterns of power in its relation to knowledge than those which lie at the local level. In the first volume of his history of sexuality, Foucault locates two broad strategies of power that dominate our age, strategies within which various knowledges have their place. These are the "anatamo-politics of the human body" and the "bio-politics of the population," the first directed toward making the human body docile and cooperative, and the second regulating and controlling human populations (Foucault 1978a, p. 139). These two strategies are, if distinct, nevertheless complementary, colluding to enact a power over life that is mutually reinforcing with, though not reducible to, capitalist development. In fact, Foucault studied the relationship between these two strategies of power as early as his history of medicine, *The Birth of the Clinic*. Now, however, these two strategies are seen to be not so much determinative for the local power relationships that occur within them as mutually reacting with and relaying across them in a pattern more complex and fragile than the early works sought to delineate.

The place of psychology in this overall pattern is within the anatamo-politics of the human body. In his history of the emergence of the prison, *Discipline and Punish*, Foucault traces several threads in the rise of psychological science and shows how it is woven into a heteronomy of practices that, at first glance, appear irrelevant to it. Among those practices were at least some that concerned punishment: how it was performed, what place it had in the social order, and how it could be accomplished better.

By the end of the eighteenth century, the question of how to treat criminality had reached an impasse. The standard form of treatment for major criminal offenses was *supplice*, translated in *Discipline and Punish* as "torture." Its intention was to reestablish the dignity of the body of the sovereign after its violation by the crime, which it did by displaying its power over the body of the criminal. Often this recoupment of sovereign integrity occurred in the form of spectacularly gruesome tortures, such as the one recounted by Foucault (1977a, pp. 3–6) that was performed on the regicide Damiens. However, two problems emerged that made this form of treatment inefficient. First, the fear that was supposed to infuse onlookers at the sight of torture often backfired into a sympathy for the object of torture. Moreover, the broadsheets that recounted the crime and the punishment, and whose purpose was to deter crime, had instead the effect of making the criminal appear more as a hero or a martyr than as an evildoer. Rather than inspiring a fear of the sovereign body's power, torture inspired a loathing for it and a solidarity with those who were its victims.

A second factor in the demise of torture was the spate of literature that called for the punitive reform. Horrified at the degradation that public torture involved, reformers demanded that methods of punishment be devised which respected rather than disgraced the human dignity of the punished. Foucault points out that this dignity which the reformers sought was not meant to signify that the criminal must be rehabilitated rather than punished; the reformers saw a criminal's humanity as something to be respected rather than altered.

But the goal of the reformers was not just to humanize punishment. Their writings occurred at a time when the threat to the social fabric was no longer from grand crimes but from smaller ones: crimes against property rather than against the social order. Punishment must not only be more humane, it must also be more efficient. It must ensure that petty criminals will get caught, rather than enjoy the toleration that a sensational but sporadic system of torture allowed. Faced with a dramatic expansion of population and the development of capitalist enterprise, the reformers saw a necessity to protect ownership that outstripped—or was coequal to—the necessity to ensure the maintenance of social order. Therefore, the blade with which the great reformers such as Beccaria and Servan cut was two-edged, subverting the ostentation of monarchical power and at the same time denying a traditional form of subsistence and economic activity to the underclasses (Foucault 1977a, p. 87).

The reformers and the populace who rebelled against torture were not a harmonious force. What the populace sought was not more authority over their lives, but less. Torture sickened them not as an inhumane form of punishment, but as the most public example of the domination under which they were forced to live. To this complaint the reformers offered not a cure but a continuation. Now, punishment was to be certain. Authority was to be reestablished not only at critical points but at every point; for, with the emergence of capitalist society, every point (being a point of private property) was critical. To see popular agitation and the reform of punishment as complementary forces is to mistake their origins and motivation. That they converged to render the practice of torture obsolete is certainly true; but they were nevertheless heterogeneous forces.

The plan of the reformers to establish a perfectly punished society was never realized. Instead of a differentiated set of punishment techniques that would deter each crime by impressing upon the mind of the public a distinct punishment to be associated with it (e.g., deprivation of civil rights for abuse of public office or fines for speculation and usury: Foucault 1977a, p. 105), one punishment became the answer to the question of all crime: namely, imprisonment.

Imprisonment was not a new form of punishment. It had been used in other countries, for instance in the Netherlands, England, and the United States. It was, however, a marginal form that did not spread until the late eighteenth and early nineteenth centuries. And when it did take hold, it embodied not only the idea of incarceration and the project of deterrence formulated by the reformers, but also a whole raft of techniques gleaned from developing forms of discipline that were being enacted at the same time as the reformist writings but in entirely different domains. Monastic enclosure and partitioning from the schools, analytical division of labor from the factories, military exercises that stressed minute body movements—all were incorporated into the development of the prison. These new forms of discipline differed from the reformers' proposals not in the idea that crime should be deterred by instilling an image of punishment in the whole of the social body, but rather in the way that such instilling should occur. Instead of preventing the body from committing a crime by the representations of punishment they offered to the mind, disciplinary techniques attempted to create a form of noncriminal mind by way of actions upon the body.

Discipline was the project of creating useful and cooperative individuals by means of minute interventions into and organization of their bodies and the spaces those bodies inhabited. *The Order of Things* demonstrated how the classical age had, in some of its empirical sciences, a schema of representation that required the drawing up of tables in order to distribute and analyze the variety of objects of knowledge. This schema was utilized by schools, the military, and factories as well: the human body was seen as a tabular grid upon which to graft the motions that one wanted to see it capable of—and oriented toward—performing. Through the use of grids and the division and elaboration of actions that were to become not only the skills but, by their encrustation onto the human body, the very character of that body, "a new object was being formed; slowly, it superseded the mechanical body—the body composed of solids and assigned movements, the image of which had for so long haunted those who dreamt of disciplinary perfection. This new object is the natural body, the bearer of forces and the seat of duration; it is the body susceptible to specified operations" (Foucault 1977a, p. 155). The new body is a docile body, a useful body, a body possessed of an empty potentiality awaiting inscription by the institutions whose task was to train it.

The methods for training the docile body, for inscribing the grid of movements that was to become the nature of this body, were threefold: hierarchical observation, normalizing judgment, and examination (Foucault 1977a, p. 170). Hierarchical observation involved the distribution of space such that the body's movements could be viewed at all times. Rather than inspecting the result of a body's production to determine whether it was adequately trained, what was required was a continuous and uniform gaze that would monitor each movement of the productive process, checking and if necessary correcting in order to achieve maximal efficiency. Normalizing judgment, a process remarked upon as early as *Histoire de la folie*, was to be carried forth by a system of rewards and punishments whose goal was to induce the body to conform to the laws of efficient movement corresponding to the activity it was being asked to perform. Here punishment consisted not of pain but of exercise; the right motions must be carved into the body by repetitive practice.[2] The examination is a combination of the other two methods; in it, the body is normalized by a power that sees without being seen. Both a ritual of power and a procedure for the establishment of truth, the examination is the culminating, if recurrent, event in the disciplinary process. Moreover, by introducing documentation into the normalizing process, the examination both constituted individuals as describable objects and opened up populations for measurement and comparative study.

It is this complex of disciplinary practices that forms the soil within which psychology took root. What is implied in disciplinary practice is the malleability of human behavior, a malleability that lies within the very functioning of the human body. Training this body, subjecting it to disciplinary processes, creates both a docile body and a set of habits and orientations that forms the initial object of psychological science. The groundwork for psychology had been laid in the writings of the reformers, since their goal was to isolate the criminal as a distinct entity separate from, and antagonistic to, the social body. Moreover, the reformers had hoped to promote habits of legality among society's citizens by installing signs of deterrence in the form of punishments to be imagined. But the emergence of disciplinary techniques changed the pole of criminal isolation and inverted the nature of deterrence. Now it was not society but normality that was offended by

2. It is often thought, even by sensitive critics (e.g., Minson 1985), that in describing the rise of such disciplinary techniques as normalizing judgment, Foucault assumed that other methods of coercion were gradually discarded. But: "The power of the Norm appears through the disciplines. Is this the new law of modern society? Let us say, rather that, since the eighteenth century, it has joined other powers—the Law, the Word and the Text, Tradition—imposing new delimitations upon them" (Foucault 1977a, p. 184).

criminal activity; and now its deterrence would not act upon the body by means of signs for the soul, but instead would create a soul by means of bodily interventions. Psychology became the executor of this normality and the custodian of this soul.

All this was accomplished through a reversal of the traditional schema of individualization, through the creation of a "descending" individualization rather than the "ascending" individualization of the feudal and postfeudal period (Foucault 1977a, p. 193). At one time, individuality had belonged to those who could afford it. Coats of arms, monuments, and elaborate ceremonies were emblems of nobility, distinguishing the aristocratic from the plebian by issuing signs of a superior individuality. Under the regime of discipline, however, it is not the noble but the abnormal that is distinguished by signs, by rituals, and by documentation. What is displayed is not distinction but deviation; the light of disciplinary processes shines on those to be watched over and, if possible, to be changed. Now it is power that resides in the shadows while its object is put under the scrutiny of the psychological gaze. "All the sciences, analyses or practices employing the root 'psycho-' have their origin in this historical reversal of the procedures of individualization" (p. 193).

Thus, the rise of psychology is inseparable from practices of power with which it has been, and continues to be, involved. The history of psychology cannot be understood solely as a progressively refined elaboration of the structure of the human mind. Neither can it be understood, as Foucault had once thought, as a conspiracy with the forces of a unitary reason against the disruption of a transcendent madness. Rather, it is the result of a complex interplay that opened up a space wherein knowledge was accreted at the same time that power was exercised. Whether this knowledge is in fact true—whether there are minds that operate in the way psychology so describes—is immaterial on this level. What is important is that the emergence of this knowledge is entwined with the exercise of this power. "It is a double process, then: an epistemological 'thaw' through a refinement of power relations; a multiplication of the effects of power through the formation and accumulation of new forms of knowledge" (Foucault 1977a, p. 224).

Psychology is not merely an ideological effect of disciplinary practices, then. And it is not reducible to the prisons it has done so much to serve. Psychological knowledge, and the practices of therapy and judgment that both derive from and contribute to it, is a distinct human science that is not epiphenomenal to any other practice. To reduce psychology to another practice is to fail to recognize that it is precisely the relationships between power and knowledge, not an identity between them, that is the object of study in Foucault's later works. And yet, to understand that psychology has a history, that it is not only the progression of an unfolding comprehension of the nature of the human mind, is to recognize that psychology, and the practices with which it is joined, not only reflects but also constructs the object it purports to study. More accurately, psychology operates at a level where the distinction between reflection and construction makes no sense. What emerges in psychological discourse, as Foucault analyzes it, is beyond the division into the reflected and the constructed, because it is beyond the division into the true and the ideological. We can say that psychology creates its object—if we understand that what is created is a knowledge that can be called neither illusory nor true, neither transcendent to discourse nor reducible to it.

What psychology creates is the soul or the mind as we know it today; and *Discipline and Punish*, a history of psychology and the practices in which it is embedded, is a "genealogy of the modern 'soul'" (Foucault 1977a, p. 29). It must be recognized that, regardless of the question of its transcendental status, the modern soul or mind is real. Beyond the ontological question of the status of the object of psychological discourse, there is a political reality created and sustained by the effective functioning of that discourse in society. Thus:

> It would be wrong to say that the soul is an illusion, or an ideological effect. On the contrary, it exists, it has a reality, it is produced permanently around, on, within the body by the functioning of a power that is exercised on those punished—and in a more general way, on those one supervises, trains, and corrects. . . . On this reality-reference, various concepts have been constructed and domains of analysis carved out: psyche, subjectivity, personality, consciousness, etc.; on it have been built scientific techniques and discourses, and the moral claims of humanism. (Foucault 1977a, pp. 29–30)

The question of the existence of the modern soul or mind can be addressed in at least two ways: ontologically, as a referent of a discourse whose reality it transcends; and politically, as the effect of discourses whose own efficacy is in a relation of mutual reinforcement with it. The answer to the first question is, from the perspective Foucault takes up, undecidable (cf. Cousins and Hussain 1984, p. 261). To the second question, however, one can reply in the affirmative. The modern soul, whatever one says about its ultimate ontological status, both exists as a profound effect of the discourses that speak of it and daily produces its own effects in the field of individual and social action. And the central discourse articulating those effects, both epistemically and politically, is the discourse of psychology. When Foucault (1977a, p. 30) writes that "the soul is the prison of the body," he is referring precisely to those constraining political effects that psychology, by being taken as a discourse with epistemic value, has had upon the body.

It is tempting to see Foucault's analysis of the emergence of psychology and the discourses allied with it as the fundamental event in the recent history of Western culture. What could be more fundamental than the modern soul and, by implication, the discourses and strategies that go into its creation? To understand things this way, however, is to commit two errors in regard to Foucault's method. The first is to assume that in this new method of analysis, which Foucault calls "genealogical," there is a discourse or practice which is central and about which all other discourses or practices revolve. Disciplinary practices did not replace but were integrated into—and in turn altered—more traditional (as well as other, capillary) discourses and practices of power.

More important, however, is that one cannot assume such a centralization of orientation without reintroducing concepts of a rule-governed unity that plagued Foucault's early writings. In describing the emergence of the disciplinary regime, Foucault warns (1977a, p. 138) that it "must not be seen as a sudden discovery. It is rather a multiplicity of often minor processes, of different origin and scattered location, which overlap, repeat, or imitate one another, distinguish themselves from one another according to their domain of application, converge and gradually produce the blueprint of a general method." The fact that disciplinary methods, and with them the discourse and practice of psychology, came to occupy an important place in Western cultural history has nothing to do either with a broad historical determinism or with the appearance of a great historical phenomenon like reason. It is a contingent fact based on the convergence of a set of dispersed practices that cannot be ascribed to a single causal mechanism. This is not to say that the rise of discipline and of psychology is accidental or that it cannot be accounted for. Rather, it is to take the small movements of history seriously. The importation of concepts such as the *a priori*, the necessary, the foundational, and the transcendental—or generalizations about broad historical processes or tendencies—in order to account for historical change and emergence pronounces in advance upon the status of our history. Such an importation says, "This can be changed, because it is accidental (or unnecessary or merely empirical); that, on the other hand, is fundamental: it cannot be changed." That psychology came to occupy the place in our society that it does today has less to do with the fate of our culture than it does with the convergence of numerous series of small practices that, had one or several of them been otherwise, might have produced a discourse very different from psychology and an object very different from a human mind or soul. The dual mistake here is to equate what is important with what is central, and what is central with what transcends the contingencies of history. Psychology is an important discourse and practice for what we are today; that does *not* mean that it is the central practice, and it does *not* mean that it is beyond the reach of a thousand small details upon which it has depended and continues to depend.

It is not enough, however, to point just to the dependence of psychology upon other discourses and practices for its emergence and its survival. For just as psychology joins in a network of practices, discursive and nondiscursive, in order to realize its effects of truth and power, so there are other networks besides the disciplinary one of prison and army, school and factory, that require it. Psychology has its effects in diverse fields and forms the nodal point for the intersection of dispersed discourses. The first volume of *The History of Sexuality* sketches another of those fields, that of sexuality, and in the course of the analysis shows how psychology emerged from and reinforced changes in that field as well.

The psychological practice that figures most importantly in the introductory volume (called in French *La Volonté de savoir*, or "The Will to Know") to *The History of Sexuality* is psychoanalysis. It is a practice about which Foucault was more ambivalent than he was about other psychological practices. In *Histoire de la folie*, for instance, he thought that psychoanalysis both liberated the discourse of madness and then, by subjecting it to the authority of the doctor, rechained it to reason. Here, psychoanalysis is credited with creating a distance between its own discourse and that of the more racialist nineteenth-century psychological discourse, while at the same time it is shown to be one of the primary tactical maneuvers in the strategy to constrain sexual behavior to an "acceptable" sexuality. In any case, psychoanalysis, like other psychological practices, has a history that must be retraced in order to discover its relationships with power and knowledge.

The history of psychoanalysis is the history of the "deployment of sexuality" as it has derived from changes in the practice of confession at the time of the Reformation and Counter-Reformation. Up until then, the objects of confessional techniques were acts, particularly sexual acts. Canon law centered upon matrimonial relations, so that sexual deviation, rather than constituting its own class, was just another type of violation of the sanctity of marriage. During and after the Reformation, however, and especially with the spread of pedagogy and medical techniques, the practice of confession began to shift its focus from violations of canon law to the thoughts and desires of the confessing individual. It was no longer the case that atonement had to do with reparations for a violation of the moral code; now one had to discover the truth about oneself of which the violation was only an expression. Now it was necessary to call upon experts, and not only religious ones but doctors, teachers, and later on psychiatrists as well, to help the individual recognize the nature of his or her soul which had produced the act. Along with this change in the status of confession, there was a change in the status of sexuality: as confession became the mode of access to the truth of an individual, sexuality—its cravings, its masks, its hidden discourses—became the truth confession sought. And in the midst of the traditional sexual bonds that centered on the family arose a foreign being, that of a new sexuality, which had to be integrated into the family in order for the family to ensure the continuance of its own structure.

The intrusion of the deployment of sexuality upon the traditional sexual arrangement of the family and its bonds (kinship structures, codes of name and material transmission, and so on) forced it to change its shape in order to accommodate this new, powerful set of practices. Although a more complete analysis of the changes produced by this intrusion is given by Foucault's colleague Jacques Donzelot (1979), Foucault points out that the deployment of sexuality entails a set of power relationships that differ from those of the family alliance. For the family alliance, power was realized on a juridical model of law, right, and possession. For the new sexuality, however, power is a matter of local and dispersed tactics that run through such nonfamilial domains as the school and the clinic.

What binds these local and dispersed tactics into a uniform sexuality is both their convergence upon an expanded set of behaviors that are considered to be sexually relevant and the development of the normality/abnormality axis to which all sexuality is now referred. At this intersection psychoanalysis finds its place, structuring the new deployment of sexuality and grafting it onto the traditional familial alliance. Indeed, the great genius of psychoanalysis lies in this: that it was able to integrate the dispersed and mobile relations of sexuality into the rigid codes of familial alliance without causing the breakdown of that alliance. Because psychoanalysis presented the deployment of sexuality as a matter of juridical power, of law—specifically the law that prohibits incest—the family, while becoming infused with sexual strategies, was able to retain a sense of itself as the focal point of those strategies and as their juridical protector. Thus sexuality, which threatened to burst the bonds of familial alliance by introducing into it new matrices of power, is coordinated with the familial scheme. Children have strange desires, it is true; nevertheless, in the end it is their parents they desire, just as their parents desire one another and their own parents.

What was being constituted in this new sexuality, which psychoanalysis sponsored and to which it owes such a great debt? Essentially, sexuality itself was being constituted, a modern sexuality that is often heralded as the deepest truth or, better, as the essence of the modern soul. As the soul was being created by disciplinary techniques, so its essence was being fashioned by sexual techniques. And in both strategies psychological thinking, psychological discourse, and psychotherapeutic intervention were drawing their nourishment and contributing their effects. In both strategies, moreover, certain social figures were being created, figures that correspond to contemporary networks of power and that invite contemporary modes of intervention—often psychological intervention. In prisons, the figure of the delinquent emerged, a criminal not in the mere authorship of a crime but in an existence that was itself deviant. The delinquent "is not only the author of his acts . . . but is linked to his offense by a whole bundle of complex threads (instincts, drives, tendencies, character)" (Foucault 1977a, p. 253). As such, the delinquent requires observation, intervention, and rehabilitation—or, if these things fail, at least surveillance and usefulness for intervening with other delinquents.

Modern sexuality has its own figures, too. Foucault (1978a, p. 105) isolates four of them, which correspond to four modes of sexual intervention into the family: the hysterical woman, the masturbating child, the Malthusian couple, and the perverse adult. The *hysterical woman* is the result of an investigation that finds the woman's body "saturated with sexuality" (p. 104). This saturation calls for a monitoring by doctors, psychological personnel, and sociologists in order to determine what kinds of saturation are normal and what dangers this ubiquitous infusion of sexuality presents. The *masturbating child* is a sexually precocious child whose activities must be observed and disciplined in order to prevent sexual degeneration. The *Malthusian couple* is the husband and wife who are responsible to the public good for their sexuality. They take their pleasure in ways that conform with the demographic, economic, and ethical needs of the society in which they live. Finally, the *perverse adult* reveals the aberrant forms that the—now isolated—sexual instinct can take. The perverse adult is the abnormal pole of the normal/abnormal axis, the shadow figure haunting the Malthusian couple, whose behavior forms a counterpoint to theirs and whose sexual vagaries thus warrant attention, study, and when possible cure.

Modern sexuality and the modern soul or mind are products of peculiarly modern forms of power. Although operating on different registers, they intersect at various points and in various practices, one of which is psychology. Together they dictate, in large part, the nature—and the inscription within networks of power—of the modern subject. The process by which the modern subject was created, known, and constrained in its activity is one—or, better, many—in which a multiplicity of practices that were both epistemic and political intersected historically over the course of the past several hundred years. This intersection was not an end point or a goal, no more than the merging of smaller waves to form a larger one is the end point or goal of oceanic currents; yet it can be singled out, named, and accounted for historically (in its emergence) and politically and epistemically (in its effects).

We know, however, that such accounting implies that the modern subject is not reducible to any naturalistic explanation, any explanation that would account for it in ahistorical or transcendental terms. We know too that inasmuch as the modern subject is historical, it is contingent: it is not destined to be with us, or rather to be us, forever. When Foucault argues against the "repressive hypothesis," he is not merely arguing against a mistaken theory of sexual history. Rather, his argument constitutes one tactic in the whole struggle against interiority, against the notion that the subject, though often the object of power relationships, has an identity or a reserve which remains untouched by them and which it is the task of movements of social liberation to free. This struggle does not have to be, although in Foucault (as will be seen) it too often becomes, a rejection of the very fact of subjectivity or interiority. It can be—and is, if Foucault's histories are taken up without the metanarrative he provides—a struggle against holding specific, contemporary types of subjectivity as natural or transcendental entities. This can be done while leaving the question of subjectivity *per se*, as the question of the referent of the modern soul was left, undecided.

The pictures Foucault paints in *Discipline and Punish* and in the introductory volume of *The History of Sexuality* are descriptions of aspects of the formation of the modern subject through practices that are both epistemic and political. His concept of power/knowledge points to this very fact: that what is presented to us as knowledge is often entwined with power relationships and vice versa. These power relationships—creative, local, shifting, and subtle—are not the product of a project of domination of one group by another. In a conversation between Foucault and Gilles Deleuze in 1972, three years before the publication of *Discipline and Punish*, Foucault makes this clear: "The question of power remains a total enigma. Who exercises power? And in what sphere? We know with reasonable certainty who exploits others, who receives the profits, which people are involved, and we know how these funds are reinvested. But as for power. . . . we know that it is not in the hands of those who govern" (Foucault 1977b, p. 213).

If power, as Foucault conceives it, is neither exploitation nor even the possession of those who exploit, it is also not a transcendental condition lying beneath history. In fact, the juridical model of power—the liberal concept of power as a limit on freedom produced by the interplay of law and right—was, during the ascendancy of sovereign monarchy, an enlightening description of the functioning of power. However, it is no longer. Power relationships, and the functioning of power in those relationships, are historical. When Foucault uses the term "power," it must be understood that, although in one sense what he speaks of—i.e., constraint upon action—has been inseparable from all of human history, in another sense (which he often fails to distinguish from the first sense) he is referring to a phenomenon that has arisen over the past several hundred years with the emergence of technology, of industrial capitalism, and particularly of various types of knowledge that have been enlaced with technology and capitalism.

That is why the power–knowledge relationship is so important for Foucault. It is not that knowledge can be accounted for by recourse to explanation in terms of power, for knowledge is not merely an effect of power. But knowledge and power are not unrelated: an account of either without reference to the other is simply incomplete. Rather, as Deleuze (1988) has shown, the problem Foucault understood, and which his writings are an attempt to solve, is how it is that knowledge and power can be heterogeneous and yet mutually reinforcing, with knowledge producing effects of power and power producing effects of knowledge. This problem—or at least its status as an important problem—is of recent origin. Without the proliferation of modes of access to knowledge (the general rise in literacy and public education), without the proliferation of domains of application of knowledge (public health, schools, jobs employing skilled workers), without technologies of communication, information, and education, the problem of the relationships between power and knowledge would have remained a peripheral one. An arcane power only marginally applied does not constitute a vital political problem. It is in Western society, with its peculiar level of development (in part caused by the intertwining of knowledge and power), that analyses of the relationships between knowledge and power become more pressing, and even urgent.

A general product of Foucault's analyses of specific power–knowledge relationships, as offered in *Discipline and Punish* and in the first volume of *The History of Sexuality*, is the images of society that appear through them. We have already seen, at least in their relevance to psychology, some specific products of these analyses: the history of the emergence of the modern soul and of modern sexuality, the figures that help both to create and to define the soul and sexuality, and the place of psychology in developing from and contributing to all this. These are the most important, though often most neglected, products of Foucault's histories. However, general images of Western society, as seen from the perspective of Foucault's specific analyses, coalesce as those analyses are carried out; and although Foucault does not intend them to be the exhaustive or exclusive pictures they are so often taken to be (e.g., Philp 1983, Merquior 1985), they do constitute at least a partial reflection of what we have become.

Those images are two: the disciplinary society and the bio-political society. The "disciplinary society" (Foucault 1977a, p. 209) has emerged from the profusion and generalization of disciplinary practices. As techniques of discipline developed in different sectors of society, they became mutually reinforcing and often consciously coordinated, so that now Western society is suffused with overlapping and complementary techniques of discipline. The contemporary world is no longer merely subject to various regimes of discipline; discipline has become a way of life. So too with bio-politics. At one time the ultimate power held over life was the threat of death. Now life itself is manipulated, not only genetically but physically and psychologically as well. Knowledge and power combine to infuse into living beings constraints to which previous ages had not been subject.

Among the relationships of power and knowledge that suffuse our society, those surrounding the discourse and practice of psychology are among the most pervasive:

> The repressive role of the asylum is well known: people are locked up and subjected to treatment—chemical or psychological—over which

they have no control; or they are subjected to the nontreatment of a straitjacket. But the influence of psychiatry extends beyond this to the activity of social workers, professional guidance counselors, school psychologists, and doctors who dispense psychiatric advice to their patients—all the psychiatric components of everyday life which form something like a third order of repression and policing. This infiltration is spreading throughout society. (Foucault 1977b, pp. 228–29)

In the peculiarly modern forms of power that Foucault analyzes, the discourse and practice of psychology—coercive without being violent, oppressive yet not ideological, the product of professional initiative more often than state decree, operating through personal attempts at self-understanding and self-improvement—is a perfect vehicle for the transmission and sustaining of a network of small practices of domination.

Although it would be absurd to reduce all modern power to the psychological, the failure to recognize the role of psychology in the contemporary field of power and domination neglects the significance of one of the most important aspects of the functioning of modern power itself. It is also to neglect the nature of the resistance required in order to struggle against the forms of domination that modern power promotes. For if domination is no longer solely a matter of state totalitarianism or economic exploitation, if it is also a matter of how we know ourselves and the world we inhabit, then it is entirely possible to overturn state power or even economic relations without altering fundamentally the domination those institutions and practices were supposed to represent. Moreover, the efficacy of transgression as a strategy of resistance is called into question when power is no longer a game of "inside" and "outside" but instead a network of small interlocking practices that are diffused across the social space.[3]

What is required, if we are to grasp the operation of modern power and the ways it can be resisted (where it needs to be resisted), is a recognition that it is not only domination but knowledge that is at stake, not only what we are forced to become but what we make of ourselves and our world. As the histories of psychology in Foucault's later works have shown, to investigate the functioning of power is often to investigate the functioning of knowledge as well; a genealogy of psychology opens out onto a critique of

3. "[T]o conceive the category of the sexual in terms of the law, death, blood and sovereignty—whatever the references to Sade and Bataille, and however one might gauge their 'subversive' influence—is in the last analysis a historical 'retro-version' " (Foucault 1978a, p. 150).

knowledge in the same gesture as it opens out onto a critique of power. And to understand the depth of the critique of knowledge, it is necessary to understand not only the specific types of knowledge that are being held up for scrutiny, but also the implications of this scrutiny for the status of our knowledge as a whole.

4

FROM PSYCHOLOGY TO FOUNDATIONALISM

Psychology is a petty science. It does not concern the problems that are most vital or urgent in our world—hunger, state terror, nuclear weapons, economic and political exploitation—but contents itself with trying to understand and, along with its allied therapies, to rehabilitate people's minds. Moreover, inasmuch as its discourse is a general one in our culture, it spreads its pettiness among us: "Concern yourself not with other things, but with yourself. Find out who you are, and what you can make of yourself. You can't change the world: but you can, if you understand yourself, adjust better to it." If Foucault's writings have taught us anything, however, they have taught us that it is often petty sciences and petty practices like those of psychology that must be investigated if we hope to understand the problems, large and small, that plague us in our present.

First of all, while not comparable to the stature of the practices of the state or religion, the discourse of psychology is part of a network of discourses that have shaped our culture. Who we consider ourselves to be, what activities we find acceptable and unacceptable, who we reject and why, how we lead our private lives and even what we consider private and what public—all are derivatives of a network of discourses and practices of which psychology forms an important part. This network helps to structure the behaviors, both individual and group, upon which the state and other "grander issues" in large part depend. Our soul and our sexuality—certainly less petty affairs than psychology by itself—are not matters of indifference in understanding what is happening in our world.

Second, the attempt to address "grander issues" without understanding their dependence upon smaller and often ignored practices is a dangerous one. History has offered us too many revolutions from the top—the state, religion, large geographic areas—that have merely reenacted the domination they proposed to abolish. We must wonder whether there are practices at the bottom that sustain such domination and that call for their own specific types of analysis and resistance. The creative powers at the extremities that Foucault analyzes are hardly less ripe for examination and often for elimination than the negative, repressive centralized powers with which they interact.

Third, the very terms in which "grander issues" are thought are often products not of the givens of human life, but of the historical practices within which they have come to be framed. This is the central lesson of genealogy. What we take for granted when we think about our present— those things we consider transcendental, *a priori*, or necessary—are themselves often products of an arcane and ignoble history, as is our presumption that they are the givens of thought. If psychology is a petty science, those objects it has helped to create—soul, sexuality, subjectivity—surely are not. They are among the foundations of our thought. And if those foundations are the product of histories which render them inseparable from relations of power and domination, then it is impossible to think that we can ignore the small, dispersed practices which give rise to them and to the "grander issues" that are articulated on their basis. To want to liberate sexuality without understanding the relationships of power embedded in the very concept of "sexuality," to seek prison reform without understanding the implications of rehabilitation, to speak in terms of the state and its subjects without inquiring into subjectivity (and as well into statehood: cf. Foucault 1981), is to repeat relationships of domination rather than to abolish them.

The genealogical critique of psychology offers an understanding of these issues: who we think we are, how our larger practices depend on smaller ones, and what dangers lie in some of the terms we use to found our thought. Psychology is not the only route to take in thinking about these issues; indeed, the investigation of psychology is possible only by recourse to related and intersecting fields which themselves could have provided the perspective we have allotted to psychology. Penology, medicine, economics, and perhaps even a stricter science like biology would have sufficed. But there is more to the critique of psychology than this. For if a history of the emergence of psychology has raised questions about some of the givens of our thought, givens that serve as the foundation for thought, it has also, though more subtly, raised doubts about the very space in which those foundations or givens of thought have arisen.

Like other doubts or questions Foucault raises, questions about the space of foundations for thought are historical ones. It is not the possibility of foundations *per se* that he doubts, but the historically specific space in which our culture finds its foundations: the space of interiority.

Foucault's distaste for transcendental givens of thought—metaphysical concepts that refer to entities or unities outside experience which are supposed to constitute experience's fundamental structures—runs like a leitmotif throughout his works. From *Histoire de la folie* through *Care of the Self*, concepts that present themselves as the foundation for all thought are historicized, politicized, and problematized. They are made to appear anything but natural or obvious. Reason, man, the gaze, origin, the soul, and sexuality have all come in for a scrutiny whose goal is to render dubious various poles around which reflection has come to organize itself. Foucault's skeptical offensives have, for the most part, been local. However, they lead to a broader form of skepticism that, while not a total skepticism about the possibility of finding foundations for thought, raises doubts about the space within which philosophers have attempted to found thought for the past several centuries. That space, the space of interiority, is most radically put into question by the genealogical histories that center around the discourses and practices of psychology.

As yet, we have refrained from offering a general definition of the term "psychology." That is because in his writings Foucault's apprehension of the psychological field has changed with the evolution of his thought and also because, as has become evident, in the later writings there are no strict boundaries between psychology and other disciplines. Broadly, however, we can define psychology as those discourses and practices (or, alternatively, those practices both discursive and nondiscursive) for which the human mind or the structure of human behavior is the central transcendental given, the conceptual buttress that supports the practices. By "human mind" we do not mean anything specific; indeed, the nature of the human mind is a subject of debate within psychological circles. That human beings do have minds, that the human mind does have a nature, and that its nature is a vital component of the nature of human being itself, however, is not a subject of debate. These parameters serve to found all practices that may be called "psychological."[1]

It should be emphasized, however, that the genealogical critique, while focusing upon existing psychological practice, does not necessarily apply to all conceivable psychological practice. Foucault's histories show that the practices of psychology in our culture, in combination with other practices of our culture, have had onerous political effects. This does not imply that any psychological practice in any culture—nor even that any psychological practice in our own culture—must be oppressive. There is strong reason to believe that alternative practices labeled "psychological" will, in the historical moment in which we find ourselves, contribute to the problems already raised by existing psychological practice. That is because the general focus upon the self which psychology fosters has become deeply entwined with the projects of normalization and discipline. The argument, however, is not an *a priori* one. The problem is not with the nature of psychology but with the practices that go under its name and with the perspective to which those practices—from school psychology to personnel management to personality theory to self-development—have given rise.

Moreover, the relevance of the psychological extends not only to the local relationships of knowledge and power that Foucault has described in his histories. There is another history, one which Foucault did not write but which his genealogical histories point to, whose domain is not the prison or sexuality but philosophical reflection. That history is one of a gradual reliance on the transcendental given of psychology in order to seek the foundation, not of this or that knowledge, but of knowledge in general. Its parameters run from Descartes to Kant—i.e., during the classical age—and its product is an orientation of foundationalist thought (i.e., thought emphasizing the need for epistemological foundations) which we have not yet escaped.

It will be said that Foucault provided exactly this history in *The Order of Things*. After all, wasn't psychology a part of the transcendental aporia that sought foundations it could not achieve because of the nature of its epistemic structure? That is not what is at issue here, however. It is not epistemological

---

1. This definition of the psychological will be objected to by behaviorists and by some physicalists. Inasmuch as they do without the concept of a unifying structure of behavior that can substitute for the mind, they escape the genealogical critique offered by Foucault. However, inasmuch as they merely substitute for the mind a coherent structure of behavior separable from the outside world, they are subject to the same genealogical questions.

incoherence that vitiates what may be called "subjective foundationalism": it is politics. The genealogy of psychology questions the "purity" of a type of transcendental reflection not because it cannot be carried through consistently, but because its history is one of power as well as of knowledge. *The Order of Things*, by denying ultimate coherence, in effect denies truth to psychological discourse and knowledge. (We must distinguish here between truth, which implies that things really are that way,[2] and knowledge, which we will take—in a usage that will perhaps be more comfortable for those trained outside contemporary Anglo-American philosophy—to mean that things are taken to be that way at a certain time and place on the basis of reasons that are themselves accepted as true.) The later writings, and the implicit critique of subjective foundationalism, do not. What the later writings signify for subjective foundationalism is that its discourse is not what it takes itself to be: an ahistorical and politically neutral reflection on the foundation of all thought.

The genealogical writings are skeptical, but not in a traditional epistemological or logical sense. They do not display the incoherence of foundationalist thought by proving an internal conceptual contradiction, but instead show that the terms in which epistemology has cast itself are politically charged from the outset. In doing so, they implicate foundationalism in a network of power relationships that, by both denying its ahistorical status and belying its claims to innocence, gives pause to those who would accept its project in the terms in which it presents itself.

A sketch of the emergence of the human mind as the foundation for epistemological reflection reveals how the genealogical history of psychology that Foucault delineates in his later writings is applicable not only to certain terms which act as the transcendental givens of our thought, but moreover

---

2. This is a rather quick and cursory treatment of what is, after all, one of the central problems not only in epistemology but also in the philosophy of language. It is part of the purpose of this chapter to demonstrate that many of the interesting issues in epistemology do not concern truth but instead justification (for a fuller discussion of this, see Chapter 6, below). This is not done, however, by way of a direct argument against the epistemological significance of the idea of truth (an argument that would take matters too far afield) but, rather, by showing the prominent epistemic role played by social practices of justification. In this sense, it might be said that the most promising approach to truth that accords with such an understanding of justification would be a deflationary one, an approach that accounts for truth as an intralinguistic device rather than a substantive concept. Although deflationary accounts of truth are controversial, the present chapter might be read as offering indirect evidence for their plausibility. For an interesting deflationary approach to truth, see the anaphoric accounts offered by Grover, Camp, and Belnap (1975) and by Brandom (1988). In any case, for our purposes we need only to understand that when we take a claim to be true, we mean—at least in part—that things are the way that claim says they are.

to a whole space in which the foundations of thought itself are offered an articulation. The prominent moments in that emergence are the epistemological reflections of Descartes, Hume, and Kant; these reflections trace a path along which much of our thought continues to tread.

Descartes' *Meditations*, whose ostensible project is to prove the existence of God and of the soul, opens with an ironic passage arguing the necessity of deductive verification rather than faith. Faith is enough for those who already recognize the veracity of the Holy Scriptures, but it is not enough for those who still need to be convinced of the existence of God. For them, to argue the necessity of God based on Scripture and of Scripture based on God is futile: "they might suppose that we were committing the fallacy that logicians call circular reasoning" (Descartes 1951, p. 3). Thus, in order to introduce certainty into the reflection upon God (and by implication into all knowledge, since God is its guarantor), what is required is to give solid foundations to thought, foundations that rely not upon faith but upon that which cannot reasonably be doubted.

Descartes' procedure of methodical doubt is well known. When doubting has reached bottom, the only thing that cannot be doubted is the existence of the doubter himself. That there is someone actually performing the doubting is the one thing that cannot be denied. This truth, however, is not a logical one, as Descartes notes in his replies to the second set of objections. It is "a simple act of mental vision" (Descartes 1927, p. 186). What doubting leaves indubitable is not activity or a process, but an entity: a mind that doubts.[3] It is from this mind that doubts that all certainty, all foundation for thought, can proceed.

For Descartes, the rejection of exteriority and the turn to interiority are part of the same process. They are accomplished in the same gesture. Foundations for thought, grounds of certainty upon which all knowledge can be based, cannot be discovered in the outside world because all that appears within that world can be mistaken. They are to be sought instead within the mind, in an interiority whose existence cannot be deduced but appears as an immediately indubitable entity, a given, from which all attempts to ground knowledge—first of God, then of the outside world—must proceed. This interiority, however, is an empty one. Possessing neither qualities nor faculties, but only the functions of thinking (including, for Descartes, believing, perceiving, and willing as well as thought), it cannot

---

3. Descartes seemed to believe that all activities or processes require an entity which is their source. It occurs not only here, but in his invoking of the Evil Genius for mistaken reasoning and of God for ideas of perfection.

by itself provide the foundation necessary to derive either God or the rest of our knowledge. What is needed is a way to move from the initial intuition of interiority to a generalized process of deduction.

The way is provided by the "general principle" which can be drawn from the intuition itself: "everything which we conceive very clearly and very distinctly is wholly true" (Descartes 1951, p. 34). The guarantor of the general principle is God, whom Descartes proves at once to exist and not to be a deceiver.

The proof of the existence of God derives from the idea of perfection that the mind can conceive but not realize in its own being. Since that idea must have a source, and since that source must be capable of the perfection of its idea, then that idea must come from a perfect being—that is, from God. Moreover, the perfection of God rules out the possibility that God is a deceiver, since deceiving is an imperfection. Thus, God exists and is not a deceiver: the general principle is vindicated.

What is important about the proof of God for our purposes is its implication that although in the order of analysis interiority is prior to God, God is both ontologically prior to the interiority that conceives it and epistemologically coequal with it in order for knowledge of the world to be guaranteed. For Descartes, interiority is not the foundation of all certainty; only interiority, in combination with the guarantee of the general principle provided by God, is. There is no pure subjective foundationalism in Descartes because the mind has had to go outside itself in order to realize the epistemological foundations it seeks. Nevertheless, the mind is one of the crucial moments of the project of giving indubitable foundations to knowledge. First, it is the initial step on the path toward indubitability. Second, it is the mind's general principle of clarity and distinctness that forms the epistemological foundation for all knowledge outside that of God and the mind itself. Finally, it is through the mind that the other component guaranteeing indubitability—God—is discovered.

In *Discipline and Punish*, Foucault credited Descartes with discovering the corporeal image of man as machine, an image which formed the philosophical counterpart to the organic man of disciplinary techniques (Foucault 1977a, p. 136). Descartes should also be credited with the opposite, but complementary, discovery of man-the-mind which was equally commensurate with those techniques. If man-the-machine was what the operations of power worked on to create a docile subjectivity, then man-the-mind was the foundation of knowledge that formed the other strand in the knowledge–power network of disciplinary processes which emerged in the classical age. Psychology took root at the intersection of these two strands, growing both out of disciplinary practices that created a soul by means of a body and out of epistemological practices that understood the body by means of the soul.

In many ways, Hume's skeptical conclusions form the counterpoint to Descartes' foundationalism. Where for Descartes the mind was the guarantor of certainty through its general principle of clarity and distinctness, it is precisely the general principle of the mind's operation regarding knowledge—the principle of causality in Hume's case—that constitutes the reason to reject the mind as a foundation for knowledge. What the mind brings to appearances in order to lend them unity and coherence is what is not to be found in the appearances themselves; it is something superadded by the mind for which no justification can be given. If for Descartes appearances are brought before the tribunal of the mind and judged on the basis of the mind's codes of indubitability and clarity and distinctness, then for Hume it is the mind that is judged by appearances—and found guilty of ascribing to them that which they do not possess.

For Hume, the nature of causality is the chief problem in accounting for human understanding, because it lies at the center of all knowledge of matters of fact and yet is not given in the appearances of things. What must be understood about the belief in causality is that it is a product not of truth but of custom. There is nothing inherent in the appearances of things that lends any justification to the idea of a necessary connection—and, thus, a causal relationship—among discrete things or events. It is merely something that occurs to the mind without any insight on its part, and it is no more significant epistemologically than would be the idea, formed by someone who lived in the arctic region, that all bears are white. "Necessity . . . is nothing but an internal impression of the mind, or a determination to carry our thoughts from one object to another" (Hume 1978, p. 165). It is a belief that can be explained, but not one that can be justified.

It might be asked here whether there is some way to interweave this ungrounded belief with the other operations of the mind, so that even if this belief cannot be accounted for epistemologically, at least it might be possible to draw a picture of knowledge—by drawing a picture of the operations of the mind that produce it—showing why it is that knowledge has the contours and shape that it does. This would be in keeping with the movement of subjective foundationalism; and, indeed, it is the very route Kant takes in attempting to found our knowledge. However, this path is not Hume's. He precludes himself from taking it by developing, in accordance with his radically empiricist principles, a concept of the self too attenuated to serve as a basis even for an account of epistemological coherence, much less epistemic justification. In fact, by the time of the appendix to A *Treatise of Human Nature*, Hume had altogether renounced the idea of being able to articulate a unity called a "self." The distinct impressions associated with the unity called the "mind" are just that—distinct—and *"the mind never perceives any real connection among distinct existences"* (Hume 1978, p. 636). Thus in contrast to both Descartes, for whom the mind as a real substance had epistemological priority, and to Kant, for whom the mind as a unity lent coherence to our distinct impressions and beliefs, Hume chose instead to give up epistemological priority and coherence by renouncing the concept of mind. Because he renounced the mind as an epistemological principle, and because he no longer had access to the pre-Cartesian unities of God and faith, Hume developed instead a thought infused by skepticism that would stand as a challenge to any program of foundationalism, subjective or otherwise, that philosophers constructed over the next two hundred years.

If Descartes attempted to vindicate epistemological foundations—and Hume to doubt them—on the basis of investigations that led through the human mind, Kant tried instead to steer a course that, while also anchored in the human mind, claimed less for it than Descartes and more than Hume. Descartes' and Hume's project, which Kant abandoned, was to understand how the mind's knowledge touched upon the objects of knowledge itself. There were, for them, things outside the mind to be known and a mind that sought to know them, and in order to account for knowledge it was necessary to understand the connection between the two. Neither of them was able to offer such an account by appeal to the mind alone, although the mind formed the basis for investigation. What distinguished Descartes' success from Hume's failure in discovering a valid connection (a connection that could guarantee the truth of knowledge, given proper premises) was his appeal to an exterior figure to guarantee that connection: God.

Kant rearranged the question. Wanting, like Descartes and Hume, to discover conditions under which knowledge could be considered valid, Kant sought the principles of that validity within the mind itself. Reasoning that the mind could know objects only in the ways it was possible for it to apprehend them, rather than as they are in themselves, Kant concluded that what was required was an investigation of the mind which could yield principles distinguishing valid from invalid attempts at knowledge. Thus,

Kant distinguished ontological conditions of knowledge—conditions of how things really are—from epistemic ones—conditions of how the mind apprehends things—and then focused on the latter in order to delineate and to delimit the foundations of knowledge of the outside world. This was his Copernican Revolution: "If intuition must conform to the constitution of the objects, I do not see how we could know anything of the latter *a priori*; but if the object (as the object of the senses) must conform to the constitution of our faculty of intuition, I have no difficulty in conceiving such a possibility" (Kant 1929, p. 22). The project of the *Critique of Pure Reason*, then, is to "isolate a set of conditions of the possibility of knowledge of things . . . that can be distinguished from conditions of possibility of the things themselves" (Allison 1983, p. 13). This is Kant's "transcendental idealism;" and by its appeal to conditions of interiority alone in order to account for knowledge, it is the beginning of subjective foundationalism proper.

By means of transcendental idealism, Kant was able to take seriously Hume's claim that we have access only to appearances while at the same time he was able to locate causality in those appearances. Appearances themselves, since they are already "mental," are imbued with principles of causality. Moreover, since appearances themselves are already "mental," the principles which found those appearances—both sensible and intellectual— are valid *a priori*, because they operate without recourse to experience. They are the conditions of validity of all experience; and the sciences of those conditions—mathematics, geometry, and logic—are sciences of the *a priori* and, thus, are valid *a priori*.

Kant's idealism, then, consists not in denying the existence of the outside world, nor even in denying its efficacy in relation to our knowledge of it. Rather, it consists in claiming that the outside world, except as it is apprehended by the mind, is irrelevant for giving an account of knowledge. Subjective foundationalism is accomplished by following through the implications of the intuitively plausible claim that one cannot experience the world except by the means available to one. It does so by offering an analysis that both describes those means and ascribes them to the functions of the human mind; and here the assumption which informs Kant's analysis is manifest. Two assumptions—that experience has structures rather than regularities and, more important, that those structures are the structures of the human mind—animate the entire Kantian enterprise. This should not be surprising, considering that philosophy in the century and a half before Kant made such an assumption *de rigueur* for epistemological reflection.

Kant's Copernican Revolution was to set foundationalism firmly on the subjectivist course it was to take for the next one hundred and eighty years, until at least the decline of phenomenology. He grounded the project of giving a rational rather than religious foundation to knowledge in the place where it had begun to take hold—in the human mind—and thus succeeded in encrusting onto all reflection upon knowledge the same parameters that were being constructed in the details of the disciplinary process described by *Discipline and Punish*. While Kant was articulating structural principles of the human mind onto the project of building episiemic foundations, disciplinary mechanisms were articulating similar principles onto the human body.

It would be claiming too much to say that the attempt to ground epistemology in the structure of the mind was merely an effect of the rise of discipline; to do so would imply that philosophical reflection was epiphenomenal, a position Foucault rejects. Further, the sketch we have offered here is not a genealogy, but a more traditional history. The strand of philosophical reflection we have followed here has been isolated from its surrounding practices. To reduce it to another set of practices, just as to make the opposite claim that it has an integrity which is irreducible to them, is to assume unities or rules where they cannot be found empirically. What is suggested by this sketch of the rise of subjective foundationalism is not that the transcendental grounding of knowledge is an ideological residue of power relationships, nor that it participated in the same strategy that psychotherapy does (although that would be an interesting genealogical investigation). Rather, the suggestion is that subjective foundationalism shares with psychology the key concept of a mind with structures and is therefore open to the mistrust that the genealogy of psychology generated toward psychological practice. Subjective foundationalism, inasmuch as the concept of a mind is at the base of its project, is to be evaluated not only in epistemological or logical terms, but in political terms as well.

With a difference, however. For psychology, the implications of a political analysis are twofold: that its knowledge participates in relationships of power and that it therefore cannot be seen as a merely disinterested field of knowledge. At least the latter implication holds true for subjective foundationalism, since the concept of the human mind it assumes has arisen at least in part on the basis of nonepistemic practices. But another, more disturbing implication appears as well. Whereas for psychology there is always the option of the turn to some sort of epistemological foundation which provides it sanctuary in the case of a skeptical attack, when the foundation itself comes under question there is nowhere else to turn. The psychologist can say, "Of course, there is such a thing as a mind; knowledge would be impossible without it." The epistemologist has no such recourse, however. To cast a skeptical net over the mind in the way that Foucault has cannot be responded to by a repetition of its status as a foundation for knowledge, because that is exactly what has been put into doubt—not by argumentation against its epistemological efficacy, but by an argument about the place of mind-oriented discourse in contemporary society. If the terms in which we cast the debate about knowledge are at once political and epistemological, then the claim that the mind is an epistemically neutral concept fails. This is not because Foucault's analyses argue directly against the existence of the mind, but rather because no neutral place can be claimed for it, no place divorced from the contingencies of our specific political, linguistic, and epistemological culture that would provide the resources which subjective foundationalism requires. If such a foundationalism is to lay claim upon our belief, the terms in which it is cast must be sufficiently removed from the concerns of our current context that we can be assured that those concerns are nothing more than a mirror of the world. What Foucault's histories demonstrate is the impossibility of such an assurance.

Foucault's position renders impossible the attempt of the epistemologist to offer a satisfying account of subjective foundationalism. For even if the case for it could be proved, it would provide a foundation whose implications are of a piece with the disciplinary society. And who would feel easy knowing that the final ground of justification for his or her knowledge also provides a means for normalizing judgments and the creation of delinquency and perversity? Indeed, it can be asked whether anything at all can constitute a proof of subjective foundationalism: If a proof lays all suspicions to rest, what evidence will lay to rest the suspicion that what is at issue in this case is not just knowledge but power as well?

The ultimate epistemological question here is not just one of the status of certain taken-for-granted "truths." It is one of whether, in the end, claims of knowledge can be justified at all. Justification has two components: the inferential move that is made—the logical step itself—and the status of the claim that is supposed to be justifying for the claim in question. Foucault's critique has nothing to do with the issue of inferential moves; even including his use of the term "reason," he has never been skeptical about logic or inference. Rather, what he promotes is a skepticism, based on political considerations, about one of the spaces in which justification has often been thought to come to an end: the space of interiority, of the mind. While abiding the movement of inference itself, he has raised doubts about one of the central places where, it had been thought, it could come to rest.

This, however, is a radical enough skepticism. For if a final ground of justification—*the* final ground in many cases—is lost to us, then what separates that which we can justify from that which we cannot? How can we say that this discourse or claim is justifiable and that one is not, if not from some foundation which is accepted by everyone? Even if our foundations turn out to be false, and other ones to be true, must there not be some foundation if knowledge is to avoid lapsing into incoherence? And if it is not to be subjective foundationalism, what else can it be? Indeed, what foundations do we have that do not somewhere employ the concept of a mind, a soul, or subjectivity? Won't our knowledge look very different if we can no longer rely on these concepts to provide a foundation for its justification? And if this foundation can be taken away from us, what about others that have not yet undergone a political scrutiny? Does the genealogical project lead ultimately to a nihilism regarding knowledge?

And what about Foucault's own claims? How will he justify his own discourse, the discourse of subversion? What grounds can he provide?

5

THE EPISTEMOLOGY
OF GENEALOGY

"Perhaps, too, we should abandon a whole tradition that allows us to imagine that knowledge can exist only where the power relations are suspended and that knowledge can develop only outside its injunctions, its demands and its interests. Perhaps we should abandon the belief that power makes mad and that, by the same token, the renunciation of power is one of the conditions of knowledge. We should rather admit that power produces knowledge (and not simply by encouraging it because it serves power or by applying it because it is useful); that power and knowledge directly imply one another; that there is no power relation without the correlative constitution of a field of knowledge, nor any knowledge that does not presuppose and constitute at the same time power relations. These 'power–knowledge' relations are to be analysed, therefore, not on the basis of a subject of knowledge who is or is not free in relation to the power system, but, on the contrary, the subject who knows, the objects to be known, and the modalities of knowledge must be regarded as so many effects of these fundamental implications of power–knowledge and their historical transformations. In short, it is not the activity of the subject of knowledge that produces a corpus of knowledge, useful or resistant to power, but power–knowledge, the processes and struggles that traverse it and of which it is made up, that determines the form and the possible domains of knowledge" (Foucault 1977a, pp. 27–28).

The foundations of much of our knowledge—those subjective foundations whose locus is the human mind—are bound to a project which is at least as political as it is epistemological. This fact, however, imposes a burden on the discourse that reveals it. For if such a discourse is not to be grounded in (i.e., not to be justified by) the foundations it has put into question, then what will justify it? What can we accept that will ground a discourse which has put so much of what we accept into question?

Foucault's archaeological work excluded the very possibility of grounds; all archives were subject to rules that rendered the search for epistemic grounds futile. There could be no question of justification, because there was no place from which justification could occur. With the genealogical studies we confront a different type of project. The question is no longer one of epistemological purging, but is instead one of specific detailings of specific problems regarding specific spaces of foundation.

If genealogy is to offer epistemic justification, then, it has three avenues open to it: to find another foundation besides subjective foundationalism, to reject foundationalism without rejecting the notion of giving grounds, and to reject the very idea that grounds can be given. Only the last option was open to archaeology, which is what made the question of grounds the one that "embarrasses me more" than other objections (Foucault 1972a, p. 205). And yet, it is often held to be the avenue chosen by Foucault even in his later works, and that by sympathizers and detractors alike. Not only contemporary Critical Theorists (Habermas, Dews, Taylor), but also those who would defend Foucault against them, often claim for genealogy the subversion of the very possibility of truth, and thus of the ability of one claim to justify another. Says William Connolly: "his genealogy of the will to truth is not itself a claim to truth. It consists, again, of rhetorical strategies designed to incite the experience of subjugation in those areas in which the question of truth recently has been given primacy" (Connolly 1985, p. 373).

The position Connolly ascribes to Foucault is, in the end, a nihilistic one. If Foucault questions specific experiences of truth which have held us in their thrall, this is not, for Connolly, because there are other experiences which yield real truth; rather, it is to give an example of what could be done in any area where truth was claimed. Foucault merely picked a few particularly onerous and particularly striking instances of its operation. This position is not unlike a relativist one, denying in the end the very possibility of its realization. For if there is no truth, then how could we possibly know it?

Our experiences of subjugation would be no more than that: mere experiences. We would be unable to draw any lessons from them, if all lessons are equally false. But what Foucault sought was not mere experiences but historical fact, "the possibility of a discourse which would be both true and strategically effective, the possibility of a historical truth which would have a political effect" (Foucault 1980a, p. 64).

If Foucault did not deny truth,[1] either to his own genealogical works or to the discourses he attempted to subvert through them, then the question of epistemic grounds becomes more urgent. For as it is wrong to say that Foucault denied the possibility of foundations for discourse *tout court*, so it is equally wrong to say that Foucault thought he could provide better or truer epistemological foundations. Foucault did not raise questions about the soul or subjectivity in order to show that they masked a deeper reality which it is the task of philosophers or political scientists to discover. He wanted us to stop looking for an ultimate truth behind the appearances that will give them a proper articulation once and for all.

Nevertheless, if we are not to say that all claims are equally arbitrary, that some histories are more accurate than others, we must somehow, in the absence of transcendental foundations, account for how it is that a discourse can be epistemically justified. We need to know not only what the political effects of a discourse are, but in addition what reasons we should have in order to commit ourselves to the idea that the facts, as stated, really are the facts, and why the interpretations of those facts are not only useful but accurate. Otherwise, as Peter Dews points out, "if Foucault is claiming truth for his historical theories, while at the same time insisting on an immanent connection between truth and power, he can only be claiming recognition for the particular system of power with which his own discourse is bound up" (Dews 1987, p. 215).

We must begin by drawing a distinction that Foucault neglected in his epistemic inquiries: the distinction between justification and truth in an ultimate sense. What Foucault must offer, in light of the radical questioning of subjective foundationalism which his genealogies have produced, is an account of how it is that we can accept his inquiries as justified, and possibly as true, given the questions he raises about subjective foundationalism and also his reluctance to support other foundationalist schemata. He does not

---

1. It is important to recall here that to be committed to truth does not necessarily commit one to some kind of correspondence relationship between words and the world. It is merely to be committed to the idea that when one says "It is true that *p*," then one is committed to *p*; that is, one believes that *p* really is the case.

have to convince us that his analyses are true in any sense beyond their justifiability; he does not, for instance, have to show us—as philosophers have so often tried to do—that his claims are somehow beyond question as an account of the way things are.[2] All he must show us—but he must show us this—is that his analyses can be justified, that we have reason to take them as true pending further inquiry. In other words, Foucault does not have to offer a foundationalist metanarrative of his genealogical writings; he does, however, have to tell us how we can justify his discourse without one.

Unfortunately, we have no *Archaeology of Knowledge* of the later works. Although Foucault often discussed his new concept of power, his attempts to offer an epistemic grounding for the genealogical works are far more scarce than one would have hoped from someone who put so much of our own epistemic grounding into question. In fact, he offers only two sustained methodological reflections on the epistemology of genealogy: a paragraph, quoted in full at the outset of this chapter, on the relationship between power and knowledge; and his 1971 essay "Nietzsche, Genealogy, History."

In the passage from *Discipline and Punish*, Foucault contrasts two pictures of knowledge. One is the traditional liberal view, which holds that knowledge occurs in the absence of relations of power; the other is the genealogical view, which sees knowledge arising as a product of power/knowledge. From the traditional perspective, the subject of power lies at the source of knowledge, giving rise to knowledge and subsequently to power: hence, subjective foundationalism and the importance of the mind. For genealogy, on the other hand, the subject comes later; it is a product of power–knowledge relationships, of the matrices formed by the interplay between knowledge and power, not their source.

Knowledge appears in this model in two places: at the source and as the product. Knowledge and power give rise to domains of knowledge as well as to subjectivity. How they give rise to subjectivity, in the form of the modern soul, has already been seen. How, then, do they give rise to knowledge itself? How can knowledge be both source and product of itself?

We must resist the temptation here to take Foucault's term "knowledge" to refer either to ultimate truth or to the totality of what is known at a given time. Neither transcendence nor totalization is at work here. It is hard to

---

2. We reserve the notion of "ultimate truth" for the traditional philosophical conception of a truth which constitutes an epistemic foundation, as opposed to the more pedestrian, and perhaps deflationary, concept of truth discussed above in Chapter 4, note 2. Maintaining the distinction between these two senses of truth, as well as the distinction between them and justification, avoids confusions that, as will be seen below, found their way into Foucault's work.

imagine that Foucault could ever understand knowledge in the first, more transcendental, sense. Nor is Foucault referring to the totality of knowledge at a given period as being either the source or the product of knowledge. After the archaeological works, such a view of knowledge as something that could be talked about *en masse* violates his program of specific analyses within specific domains.

What Foucault means when he finds knowledge both at the source and as the product of knowledge is that specific domains of knowledge combine with specific domains of power in order to yield other specific domains of knowledge (and of power). It is, for instance, the combination of disciplinary techniques and the classical concept of the body that gave rise to the descending individualization which is the source of psychology; or the combination of Reformation confessional practice and medical knowledge that gave rise to the domain of sexuality. Thus, it is not a question of knowledge giving rise to itself, but rather one of the inseparability of knowledge and power in the production of any given domain or field of knowledge.

However, to the question of how such a view of power–knowledge relationships can be justified epistemically, of how one can know that this is the case, there is nothing in the passage to provide an answer. This is undoubtedly because Foucault thinks his histories serve as the answer; and there is truth to that line of reasoning. The histories do articulate instances in which practices of power and knowledge give rise to other practices of knowledge. Still, it leaves two matters unresolved. First, Foucault's historical analyses are specific and, thus, do not allow for a generalization from the analyzed cases to cases not examined. Foucault can claim from his historical analyses that certain knowledge—for instance, knowledge of the modern soul—arises in the way he has shown; but he cannot claim that those analyses can serve as a general picture for all knowledge. This limitation is not a deep one for his project, but rather a delimiting of its boundaries, and there is reason to believe that Foucault would probably accept it.

The more disturbing question, however, is this: How can Foucault argue that the picture of the relationship between knowledge and power he has painted is a valid one, *even in specific instances*, unless he offers a means for justifying the validity of that picture? Without such means, he cannot claim that the knowledge about which he speaks—as well as the knowledge in the name of which he speaks—is anything more than ideology. If knowledge cannot be justified, if it cannot be spoken of in epistemological as well as political terms, then, as Peter Dews has pointed out, it is merely an effect of relations of power.

What Foucault needs, and what he attempts to provide in his essay "Nietzsche, Genealogy, History," is a description of genealogy that will allow it to be accounted for as an area of knowledge. Once it is understood how genealogy is an epistemological matter as well as a political one, then it will be clear how, in the absence of foundationalist schemata, Foucault sees knowledge—and, most important, his knowledge, the knowledge which genealogy provides—as capable of justification.

"Genealogy," he says, "is gray, meticulous, and patiently documentary. It operates on a field of entangled and confused parchments, on documents that have been scratched over and recopied many times" (Foucault 1977b, p. 139). Genealogy works slowly, in the details of history, in order to discover how a discourse or a practice arises and comes into prominence. Yet, to trace the rise of a discourse or practice is not to seek its origin. An origin is that single source which provides both the material and the motivation for the flowering of a discourse or practice: it is the glorious womb. The concept of origins, however, involves three mistakes that genealogy corrects. First, it assumes an essence behind the phenomena, a being behind the becoming. Second, it assumes that historical beginnings are grand affairs, when more often than not they are lowly and dispersed. Last, it imports a notion of truth—even ultimate truth—into beginnings: the origin is the foundation of a discourse, its pristine instant, its moment of pure communication with itself. In fact, truth—all truth[3]—is not so much a purity which can be opposed to error as "the sort of error that cannot be refuted because it was hardened into an unalterable form in the long baking process of history" (Foucault 1977b, p. 144). Truth itself requires a history—not a history of its progressive unfolding or of the obscuring of its original face, but a history of its creation and re-creation over time.

If genealogy does not seek origins to account for the rise of its objects, it engages instead in a twofold task: *Herkunft* and *Entstehung*, "descent" and "emergence." Descent and emergence are two complementary historical methods that merge to form a history without unity, goal, or origin. Descent recognizes that unity derives from a dispersion of singular events. Rather than accounting for a discourse, a practice, or even an event in terms of the origin which is its source, descent looks at separate events in unrelated

---

3. On the distinction, which Foucault at times elides, between truth and what we have called "ultimate truth," see note 2, above.

domains to see how these have come together to form the object of genealogy's investigation. The soul, once thought to be a transcendent unity, is shown in the tracing of its descent to be a coincidence of dispersed discourses and practices. Morality, too, is the product of various lowly and often ignoble practices. If there is a unity to be found in descent, it is only that of the body, which is the surface upon which the dispersion of events is inscribed in order to form the unities that present themselves to appearance.[4]

Emergence is complementary to descent. It recognizes that the movement of history is not a progress or a development but a play of forces each struggling for dominance, forces which change with the history that is their product. Emergence traces the "hazardous play of dominations" (Foucault 1977b, p. 148) of the forces of history, a play that has no goal or progress. The illusion of progress is only an interpretation grafted onto history by the force that is dominant (or by the structure of forces, both dominant and dominated) at the moment the interpretation is offered. Far from being the realization of a meaning or the intention of a force transcendent to it, history is the anonymous play of forces that, in their dispersion, are under no one's control and have no common end in view. And so, "[a]s it is wrong to search for descent in an uninterrupted continuity, we should avoid thinking of emergence as the final term of an historical development" (p. 148).

Genealogy, then, traces the play of dispersed forces as they form shifting and dissolving unities which have no purpose or intention informing them. And knowledge, too, rather than lying behind this movement, is part of it. In the course of his account of genealogy, Foucault twice accuses knowledge as being a sort of error: it is the error of the origin which comes to be accepted as true, and it is the false interpretation of progress which the play of dominations gives itself in its meaningless march through time. Does this mean that all knowledge is false? That would be too facile. What it means, rather, is that knowledge is one of the stakes in the struggle by various forces for domination. How history—and not only history—is perceived, what its meaning is taken to be, how it is to be understood, are not products of an intelligence operating at a distance from its object; they are the products of a struggle and an emergence. And knowledge changes, often in the form of discontinuous breaks, not because new discoveries have been made but

4. Minson (1985) points out that Foucault's concept of the body as a material upon which the operations of power are performed is a reversion to transcendental thinking. Genealogy, since it treats power as positive and productive, does not require a substratum to account for unity; the notion of the transcendent body, then, is a gratuitous concession to transcendental thought (see esp. pp. 92–97).

because there is a shift of forces which has resulted in a new appropriation of knowledge and, thus, a new set of interpretations which are now called truth. It is this struggle around knowledge, this struggle to construct interpretations which are to be taken as true, that Foucault calls "the will to knowledge."

The will to knowledge is not merely a desire to know, a desire for understanding, although it is that too. Entwined with this desire for understanding is a desire for appropriation, a desire to seize the means of understanding and to mold them into an interpretation. Thus, since knowledge and interpretation are inseparable (indeed, all knowledge *is* an interpretation), the distinction between wanting to know and wanting to impose an interpretation cannot be made. In the inaugural lecture at the Collège de France, Foucault (1972a, p. 219) saw the will to knowledge as essentially a negative, constraining force. In "Nietzsche, Genealogy, History," however, though written at about the same time, there is another, more positive aspect to the will to knowledge; it is not merely a force of exclusion through the prohibitions of falsity, but a positive phenomenon as well, creating interpretations and molding history in the same gesture with which it marginalizes and exiles. The will to knowledge is a domination that is at the same time an interpretation.[5] Knowledge does not stand outside the fray in order to pronounce its truth; it is not an observation from above, but a weapon used below: "knowledge is not made for understanding; it is made for cutting" (Foucault 1977b, p. 154). And genealogy is the record of those forces which have had their hand upon the knife.

That is why genealogy is *wirkliche*, an actual and effective history. Genealogy is a history without constants, tracing not developments but struggles, not the reconciliation of knowledge and things but the violent appropriation of interpretation, not the process of coming to fulfillment but the processes of contingent unities and dispersions. For the genealogist, the epistemological lesson of history is "its affirmation of knowledge as perspective" (Foucault 1977b, p. 156). There is no outside from which to view history, since all history is a struggle.

And this is true for the genealogist as well as for others. The task of genealogy is not to recount history in its purity, but to give another perspective to history, one whose purpose is to rid history of its illusions of progress and reconciliation. Genealogy is a "curative science" (Foucault

---

5. The editor of the English translation of the essay notes that the French term Foucault uses for "the will to knowledge," *vouloir-savoir*, "means both the will to knowledge and knowledge as revenge" (Foucault 1977b, p. 163).

1977b, p. 156), taking on the task of subverting the assurances of transcendence or meaning which history appears to offer to knowledge. In short, genealogy reintroduces history back into history, through a radical historicizing that leaves no corner for those who would speak in its name only to destroy it. Genealogy, like other knowledge, is a weapon, pointed at transcendence and at anything that feeds upon transcendence: origin, constituting subjectivity, *a priori* knowledge. It is the blade of history carving the moniker of relativity into all things absolute.

Conceived as such, genealogy is an epistemological failure. By grounding genealogy in historical relativism, by introducing the concept of a will to knowledge whose most important project is always something other than knowledge, Foucault in effect rejects the distinction between knowledge and power that infuses his historical analyses; he reduces all knowledge to power, and thus to ideology. When genealogy becomes a discourse to be judged solely as a weapon and without regard to its epistemic justification, it undercuts its own usefulness even as a weapon; there can be no accurate genealogy, as opposed to an inaccurate one, and thus no need for a "patience and a knowledge of details" (Foucault 1977b, p. 140). The genealogical project, as a project of relativizing knowledge to the play of forces, runs up against the same obstacles that confronted archaeology when it relativized knowledge to rules and archives. In both cases, knowledge is no longer an epistemic project; and, thus, the epistemic assent requested by the analyses which hold it as their object, be they archaeological or genealogical, is precluded at the outset. The arguments of the Critical Theorists that Foucault's genealogy has no place to stand, having undercut any place knowledge could give an account of itself as knowledge, seem to be correct.

And yet, unlike the case of archaeology, Foucault's genealogy possesses an ambivalence that resists reduction to epistemological relativism. His histories are patiently local and rarely generalizing. His treatment of power/ knowledge in *Discipline and Punish* showed knowledge to be not merely product but also source. In a late interview, Foucault chastised those who, "[w]hen you point out to them that there can be a relation between truth and power, they say: 'Ah, good! Then it is not the truth' " (in Bernauer and Rasmussen 1988, p. 17). How are we to understand, then, his "reduction" of knowledge to a play of forces? How are we to make sense of this relativist account of genealogy which rejects the subtle articulation given to knowledge in Foucault's histories?

Foucault is ambivalent about the epistemic status of his own texts, vacillating between holding them to be true—or at least justified—analyses and seeing them as subverting the very possibility of a true or justified analysis. This ambivalence precluded him from providing the epistemic ground he needs in order to realize his project. It is an ambivalence that derives not solely from his own work but that, in part, was inherited from his predecessor in genealogy: Nietzsche.

Nietzsche's influence upon Foucault shimmers across the surface of each of Foucault's texts. "I am simply Nietzschean, and I try to see, on a number of points, and to the extent that it is possible, with the aid of Nietzsche's texts—but also with anti-Nietzschean theses (which are nevertheless Nietzschean!)—what can be done in this or that domain" (Foucault 1985a, p. 9). In the early works, Nietzsche stood as the transgressor—of reason, of *epistēmē*, even of health—inscribing his madness into that serene fixity which dominant discourses attempted to impose. Alongside Artaud, Sade, and Bataille, Nietzsche articulated a transgressive discourse that disrupts without being recuperable, that disturbs the social and cultural bonds without hope of reconciliation or integration. With the genealogical turn, however, Nietzsche appears as another figure, still as disruptive but not as insane. Nietzsche is now "the philosopher of power" (Foucault 1980a, p. 53), patiently and studiously tracking down power into those interstices it has been able to occupy without revealing itself to those of lesser vision or attentiveness. *Discipline and Punish* can be read as a rewriting of the second essay of *The Genealogy of Morals*, " 'Guilt,' 'Bad Conscience,' and Related Matters," in which Nietzsche presents a history of the inscription of memory. Memory, for Nietzsche, is inseparable from punishment. And eventually it blunts the capacity for instinctual action, rendering people more calculating and reticent in regard to their instincts: "All instincts that are not allowed free play turn inward. This is what I call man's interiorization; it alone provides the soil for the growth of what is later called man's *soul*" (Nietzsche 1956, p. 217). The emergence of that interiorization, the formation of the soul, is precisely Foucault's object in his history of the prison.

If Nietzsche provided the guidance for so much of Foucault's work, some of his ambivalences and confusions have found their way into it as well. To reduce Foucault's work to Nietzsche's would of course be absurd. As Minson points out, Foucault, even when doing the most Nietzschean of histories, still departs from his teacher in significant ways: his periodizations are closer to the present, his attack upon the transcendental is less directly philosophical and, in contrast to Nietzsche, he sees psychology as a practice to be overturned rather than utilized for critique (Minson 1985, pp. 79–80). However, as Minson (1985) and Megill (1979) both point out, some of the ambivalences and tensions in Foucault's work can be traced to Nietzschean influences that Foucault appropriated without recognizing their problematic character. Not the least among these is Nietzsche's perspectivism.

That perspectivism appears most starkly in the fragments collected in Nietzsche's *The Will to Power*. "The world with which we are concerned is false, i.e. is not a fact but a fable and an approximation on the basis of a meager sum of observations; it is 'in flux,' as something in a state of becoming, as a falsehood always changing but never getting near the truth: for—there is no 'truth' " (Nietzsche 1967, p. 330). Instead, what we call "truth" is merely an interpretation imposed upon the world in the play of forces for domination. " 'Truth' is therefore not something there, that might be found or discovered—but something that must be created and that gives a name to a process, or rather to a will to overcome that has in itself no end" (p. 298). What is called "truth" is not an epistemic matter but a political one; it has to do with the interaction of constrained and constraining forces. There is no truth, if by truth is meant "the way things are," because what is accepted as the way things are is always an interpretation; and interpretation is the product of struggle, not of insight. Interpretations are imposed by force, not discovered by the understanding. And the name given to the position that understands this dynamic of interpretations is "perspectivism": "In so far as the word 'knowledge' has any meaning, the world is knowable; but it is *interpretable* otherwise, it has no meaning behind it, but countless meanings.—'Perspectivism' " (p. 267).

At first glance, this position appears to be either a nihilism or a simple self-refuting relativism, claiming that the world contains an infinity of meanings and thus that any interpretation is true only in relation to the meaning it explicates. But would not that very claim be a reduction of the world to a single interpretation? Alexander Nehamas, confronting Nietzsche's perspectivism directly, argues that what Nietzsche claims is not that the world itself possesses many meanings, that it contains some sort of "ontological pluralism" (Nehamas 1985, p. 64). Rather, Nietzsche denies that any ontological categorization of the world is possible. The reason the world is susceptible to many interpretations, the reason there is no truth, is that the world is ontologically indeterminate; that which interpretations are interpreting cannot be rendered in any interesting sense.

The ontological indeterminacy of Nietzsche's perspectivism is not so easily refuted as a relativist ontological pluralism would be because it does not make the same positive claims that pluralism does. The relativist, by holding that the world has many meanings, is forced to admit that the meaning which the world has on the pluralist interpretation is also only one of many meanings. To do so, however, is impossible, for if the world really does have many meanings, then there is one interpretation of the world that embraces them all—the very interpretation which claims it has many meanings. Thus, the ontological pluralism of the relativist is defeated in the very gesture by which it tries to establish itself: the world can contain many meanings, and thus be susceptible to many interpretations, only inasmuch as it sustains an embracing interpretation (corresponding to a single meaning), which is precisely what the relativist wants to deny.

Perspectivism does not suffer the same logical problem. What must be denied, and what perspectivism does deny, is not the unity of the world's meaning but "the more fundamental claim that there could ever be a complete theory or interpretation of anything, a view that accounts for 'all' the facts; we must deny the claim that the notion of 'all the facts' is sensible in the first place" (Nehamas 1985, p. 64). Perspectivism's position is not that the world contains many meanings but, rather, that every view upon the world is an interpretation, a limited and revisable perspective, and that there are many interpretations. It is the perspectives which are plural, not the world or reality itself, whose unity or plurality cannot be determined. This view, says Nehamas, is not self-refuting, because perspectivism is not an argument from necessity; it does not claim that all views of the world are *necessarily* perspectives, but only that all those which history has shown are in fact perspectives. Perspectivism is a contingent argument; therefore, its refutation would derive not from an *a priori* argument, but from an empirical one—by showing that there is a view of the world which is not perspectival, not limited and revisable. Thus, unlike the relativism Nehamas describes, which because of its ontological commitment to pluralism is self-refuting *a priori*, perspectivism can affirm itself without contradiction.

Nehamas's view of Nietzsche's perspectivism appears to be quite different from Foucault's, which affirmed perspectivism as an *a priori* matter, entailed by the fact that knowledge is the product of struggle rather than the disinterested search for truth. However, Nehamas attains such a view only at the cost of rendering his perspectivism either vacuous or incoherent. For if perspectivism claims only that all views on the world are in fact limited and revisable perspectives, then he is claiming no more than what everybody already knows: that a single, encompassing theory of the world and all its perspectives has not yet arisen or, if it has, has not been circulated very widely. But if Nehamas is claiming (and it seems he must) that Nietzsche's perspectivism is committed to ontological indeterminacy, then perspectivism must itself be an *a priori* matter and thus becomes self-refuting. Nehamas's ontological indeterminacy holds that there can be no unsurpassable analysis, that the notion of an unsurpassable analysis does not even make sense. This can be true only if all perspectives are *necessarily* limited. To make such a claim, however, is self-refuting because if they are necessarily limited, then there is one unsurpassable perspective: that of perspectivism itself.[6]

Nehamas and Foucault, then, are not so far apart as it may appear. Specific differences regarding perspectivism's argument aside, both writers hold to a general view of Nietzsche's thought that requires the *a priori* perspectivist commitments which Foucault has made. The problem with these commitments is that knowledge is reduced to something nonepistemic, and not in part but as a whole. Knowledge is no longer knowledge, because there is no longer any way that its claims can be epistemically redeemed; its claims are precluded from having an epistemic hold upon us. Not only is knowledge no longer a matter of ultimate truth or even a more pedestrian concept of truth, it is not even a matter of justification. It is an act of belief that is a pure leap of faith. But if this is so, any account of knowledge, insofar as it is meant to be taken seriously, is self-refuting, because it denies that very space of justification which it would need in order to vindicate itself.

Perspectivism blurs the distinction between epistemic and nonepistemic accounts of knowledge by reducing the former to the latter. It is certainly possible to give nonepistemic accounts of the emergence of various domains of knowledge. The history of the emergence of psychological discourses on the modern soul is a case in point. Such a history claims nothing about knowledge in general; and, although it raises suspicions concerning discourses on the modern soul which can translate into a withdrawal of immediate epistemic assent, it makes no direct claims about the epistemic status of those discourses. It is a historical account of how a certain domain of knowledge came about. However, to say that that knowledge is only a matter of that history is to make a direct epistemic claim where none was shown. Foucault is careful not to do this in his histories, but not so careful in his methodological account of genealogy. Further, to make the additional commitment to relativism or perspectivism *tout court* is to reduce all knowledge to history (or to some other variable); it is to found all knowledge

6. The claim of ontological indeterminacy is not the only place where Nehamas's reading of Nietzsche's perspectivism is required to become *a priori*. His notion of the will to power as a play of forces, if not as agonistic an interpretation as Foucault gives, also entails that perspectivism become a matter of necessity, not just contingency. See Nehamas 1985, chap. 3.

upon nonepistemic factors. This leaves the relativist or perspectivist without the possibility of epistemic appeal and, thus, with no recourse for defense of the relativist or perspectivist view.

But is Foucault the relativist his genealogical essay makes him out to be? Did he come to realize in the years between 1971 and 1975 (the publication of *Discipline and Punish*) that Nietzsche's perspectivism was epistemologically suspect? Since there are no essays on the epistemology of genealogy after 1971, this possibility is hard to confront directly. Moreover, the style of the essay is too approving of Nietzsche's genealogy to think that Foucault had serious reservations about it. But if he did approve of Nietzsche's perspectivism, then what are we to make of Foucault's denials that genealogy rejects the truth of the discourses it investigates?

At times, Foucault seemed to understand genealogy as a local tactic whose generalizability could come only from a proliferation of specific genealogies. It was in this vein that he once said, "[I]t will be no part of our concern to provide a solid and homogeneous theoretical terrain for all these dispersed genealogies, nor to descend upon them from on high with some kind of halo of theory that would unite them" (Foucault 1980a, p. 87). Understood in this way, genealogy's political import lies in its very specificity. First of all, by upsetting the "natural" order at a specific site, genealogy participates in the struggles which occur on that site, taking the side of those discourses and practices which are oppressed. The image of genealogy here is of a weapon used by the dominated to show that their domination is not a natural, but instead a historical, affair. Perversion and madness, and the soul and subjectivity by which they are proclaimed, are the product of struggles and not the givens of our thought. Second, in refusing to provide an encompassing theory or narrative within which to place these specific genealogical interventions, genealogy resists its own impetus toward totalization or transcendence.

However, this second political project of genealogy—the refusal of theory—opens onto concerns much wider than those of the specific struggles which the genealogies themselves articulate. What is at stake in the refusal of genealogy to offer a unified theory of its interventions is the very justification of political intervention itself. In the genealogical view, one cannot justify one's struggles by recourse to a single unified theory that lends coherence to all of one's actions. Even to attempt to do so is to engage oneself in discourses whose foundations are politically suspect. Foucault understood that his genealogies raise troubling questions not just for psychology or penology, but for epistemology generally. This understanding led

Foucault to offer other accounts of his thought, accounts not bound to specifics or to a mere refusal to engage broader questions. Unfortunately, those accounts, of which the most sustained is the essay on Nietzsche, lapse into relativism and the problems of self-refutation that attach to it.

There is a tension in Foucault's thought between an antifoundationalist account of genealogy—an account which refuses, by recourse to the specificity of genealogy, to address questions of justification—and a relativism which recognizes the broader implications of specific genealogical interventions but which renders them incoherent by resorting to an explanation that leaves no room for its own justification. But if genealogy is only a set of specific analyses, then how are we to understand the broad epistemological implications of its results? And, on the other hand, if those broad epistemological implications cannot be justified, how are we to understand genealogy at all? This dilemma can be seen in a passage by Foucault that admits of two very distinct readings, one epistemological and relativist and the other political and nonepistemic:

> Truth is a thing of this world: it is produced only by virtue of multiple forms of constraint. And it induces regular effects of power. Each society has its regime of truth, its "general politics" of truth: that is, the types of discourse which it accepts and makes function as true; the mechanisms and instances which enable one to distinguish true and false statements, the means by which each is sanctioned; the techniques and procedures accorded value in the acquisition of truth; the status of those who are charged with saying what counts as true. (Foucault 1980a, p. 131)

Here the concept of truth is ambivalent. If all truth (or what we have been calling "knowledge") is a thing of this world, then what of Foucault's knowledge? Is it, too, a thing of this world? If so, then, Peter Dews is right to say that in accepting Foucault we are not accepting an account of how things are, but only a politics: Foucault's politics, as opposed to the general politics of truth current in our society. Moreover, we can have no reason to accept Foucault's politics, or even to reject it, because there are no claims to which justification can appeal. However, if Foucault is not speaking of all truths, but rather of specific truths and specific regimes that inhabit each society without exhausting its epistemic stock, then the question with which this chapter opened returns: How, in the absence of a foundationalist account, can Foucault ground his own critique of these specific truths? What picture of justification can he offer which is neither foundationalist nor relativist?

The fundamental problem of genealogy is that of a neglect of the epistemological implications of a critique of knowledge. Foucault is correct to talk about the intertwining of knowledge and power as he does at the beginning of *Discipline and Punish*. (At least he is correct to point it out in specific instances—and there are many of them.) And yet, his analyses are essentially political. The lessons they teach are lessons in the politics of knowledge. The depth of those lessons, the profound way in which they cut into our knowledge, however, requires something more than a politics. They require an epistemology as well. When the old categories of our knowledge give way to a critique which while not refuting them casts suspicion upon them, then another obligation falls upon the critic besides the political one he or she has taken up. Foucault was aware of that obligation, and at times he tried to address it. But because he was more interested in politics than in epistemology, and because his interpretation (and, at times, confusion) of the concepts of truth and knowledge allowed no space for the notion of epistemic justification, his proposals regarding truth were always either too little or too much. Thus, we still face the question of how the critique of knowledge will be able in the end to vindicate itself.

6

ANTIFOUNDATIONALISM

Gilles Deleuze offers the most sustained attempt to articulate the ground of Foucault's genealogy and the relationship between knowledge and power. In *Foucault*, Deleuze considers Foucault's texts as an essentially unified work concerned primarily with the historical formation of knowledge. Foucault's early works are investigations into the various strata of knowledge that take hold within—and of—certain periods. The later works, particularly those concerned with power, provide a foundation of that view of knowledge, showing how knowledge can be both historical and stratified at a given period and yet changing across periods.

Knowledge is a matter of the relationships within a given period between the discursive and the nondiscursive, or, because the term "nondiscursive" misleadingly implies a negativity where one does not exist, between the articulable and the visible. The articulable is a matter of statements, described in *The Archaeology of Knowledge* as material entities that find their place relative to a network of other statements during a discursive formation. There is a unity among statements at a given historical epoch, the unity of the *epistēmē*, that can be described in terms of its regularities without reference to anything outside it. But to do so is to see only half the picture.

Foucault discovered, as his work progressed, that what he had called the nondiscursive was not merely an Other, unrelated to the articulable, but a positivity which, though distinct from the articulable, occupied a corresponding place with it in the formation of the stratum of knowledge in a given historical period.

The discourse of psychology is more than a moment in a historical formation of discourses. It is also decisive in the emergence of the prison, influencing the distribution of its space and the prisoners inside it. *Discipline and Punish* showed how the discourses of the body during the classical age combined with practices that operated not only through discursive but also through nondiscursive—physical or "visible"—mechanisms in order to form the psychological discourses as well as those on delinquency. It was a confluence of the articulable and the visible—or, perhaps more accurately, of articulables and visibles—that gave rise to psychology and formed a part of the *epistēmē* or historical stratum of knowledge inhabiting the postclassical age.

The visible and the articulable do not function along the same register, however. They are not two strands of a similar positivity that coincide in the formation of a specific type of knowledge or a specific historical stratum. Knowledge itself is a discursive matter, a matter of statements and not of pure visibilities. Deleuze sees it thus: there is a primacy of the articulable over the visible in that the articulable is the "determining" while the visible is the "determinable" (Deleuze 1988, p. 61). The visible is the mute materiality, the pure content that forms the backdrop against which the articulable is articulated; while the articulable itself is the expression that gives form—the form of knowledge—to the content of the visible. The articulable, though, is not in the same relation to the visible as language is to sense-data in an empiricist account of knowledge, that of a form which mirrors the content offered to it. The articulable is not a mere reflection of the visible, nor is the visible a brute physicality that determines what can be said about it. Both the articulable and the visible have their own relationships internal to them, and although in their coincidence the primacy belongs to the articulable (because it gives the form of knowledge to the visible), the two exist as parallel registers, each with its own integrity.

If, however, the visible and the articulable are not in a relation of content to form in the traditional sense, then what brings them together? How do these two different registers of knowledge coincide to form a single stratum? They do so through a "third agency" (Deleuze 1988, p. 68) which runs transversally through them: the agency of power. Power is a relationship between forces. Forces can be either active or reactive, inducing effects or performing them. What determines their activity and their passivity, though, is not their intrinsic character, but the domination that some forces have over others in a given historical period. Thus a force that is active can become passive and vice versa, which allows for the changes that have occurred historically in regimes of knowledge and of power.

The relationship between knowledge and power is like the relationship between articulation and visibility within knowledge: they are heterogeneous, yet they presuppose one another, and yet again power has a primacy over knowledge. Power's primacy over knowledge consists in the fact that it is power—i.e., the relationship between forces—which knowledge articulates when it takes the form of knowledge. The statement is "the thing that brings about or actualizes relations between forces," forces that themselves "were outside the statement" (Deleuze 1988, p. 70). Again, the relationship is not one of mirroring, but of expressing in one register something that has a different style of existence in another. The visible is also an expression of the relationship of forces, giving a form to them which is not that of discourse but instead of a visible materiality. And that is how power traverses both the visible and the articulable and brings them into communication. The same set of power relationships, of relationships between forces, can be expressed by both the articulable and the visible. They express what Deleuze calls "pure functions" (p. 33). In the case of *Discipline and Punish*, the pure function that is expressed both in the visible and in the articulable is that of panopticism: "*to impose a particular conduct on a particular human multiplicity*" (Deleuze 1988, p. 34). Here the visible and the articulable converge into a unity, the unity of expressing a particular relationship or diagram of forces that is transversal to the registers of both.

And this is why, even though knowledge is the expression and power is the content, power nevertheless has primacy over knowledge. Knowledge "would have nothing to integrate if there were no differential power relations" (Deleuze 1988, p. 81). Unlike the case of the articulable and the visible, the relationship between power and knowledge is one of foundedness: knowledge, though irreducible to power, is still founded on force relations. In this sense, it is possible to say that knowledge is founded upon power. What relations of power create are not specific truths (or, better, specific claims or theories that pass for truth in a given historical epoch), but instead "problematizations," spaces of knowledge within which certain questions arise, certain procedures for attaining truth are established, and certain visibilities and articulations are formed.

Nevertheless, although power does not create truths—or what passes for truth—doesn't the Deleuzian rendering fall into the same relativist self-refutation that Foucault fell into with his Nietzschean rendering of genealogy? Isn't the historical relativization of the problematization of truth, though more subtle than the historical relativization of truth *per se*, the same sort of totalization of knowledge that is unable to cite its own grounds for totalizing? This would seem to be the case. However, Deleuze introduces another procedure, distinct from knowledge, that has the capacity to grasp the founding procedures of power as well as the visibilities offered to knowledge: thought. "If seeing and speaking are forms of exteriority, thinking addresses itself to an outside that has no form. To think is to reach the non-stratified" (Deleuze 1988, p. 87). Unlike knowledge, which is a stratum formed by the intersections of statements and visibilities, thought reaches the relationships of force that subtend and traverse historical strata. Thought is something other than knowledge, delving beneath it in order to understand the forces upon which it is founded, the content it expresses.

Thought is not caught in the nets of historical relativism. This does not mean that thought itself does not change with time; it changes with the changing shape of the force relationships it is trying to understand. But thought is always "thought from outside," as a Foucault article on Blanchot was entitled (Foucault 1987); thought reaches beyond what is given to it in the mutually implicated exteriorities of the visible and the articulable to the diagrammatic relationships that cut across them and make them possible. That is why Deleuze (1988, p. 51) can say without relativist self-refutation: "there is therefore nothing behind knowledge (although, as we shall see, there are things outside knowledge)." It is also why Deleuze (p. 84) contradicts Foucault, finding micropolitical relationships not only in the classical and postclassical epochs, but all throughout history. The microphysics of power inhabits not only the more recent *epistēmēs*; in all *epistēmēs*, power traverses knowledge in diagrammatic ways (of which panopticism is only the most recent). The project of thought is to comprehend those diagrams.

Thought is the return of the epistemic to its status as an irreducible in relation to power. Thought grasps power because it is not merely its expression (even if knowledge, while an expression of power, is still heterogeneous from it). However, although Deleuze distinguishes thought from knowledge, this is not finally the distinction he is after. For if knowledge were not also thought of its own object—i.e., the attempt to understand what founds it beneath its own exteriorities—it would no longer be knowledge but, once again, only ideology. And if thought were not also knowledge—offered in the language of and according to the comprehensibility of a certain time and place—then it would have no choice but to remain mute: indeed, one wonders how it would ever get started at all. The distinction Deleuze is making here is not between knowledge and thought, but between the object of genealogy and genealogy itself, between knowledge (or thought) taken as an object of genealogical study and knowledge (or thought) taken as an attempt to think genealogically, in terms of the power relationships inhabiting various practices of knowledge. Deleuze introduces an epistemological concept at the point where his rendering of knowledge–power relationships threatens to become self-refuting, and for good reason: genealogy itself is not reducible, at least (and this will turn out to be crucial) not in the moment of its analysis, to the same form of power relationships in terms of which the object of its investigation is articulated.

What Deleuze has understood is that the essay on Nietzsche is not enough to ground genealogy, because it reduces genealogy itself to an expression of power. What is required—and Deleuze appeals to Foucault's article on Blanchot to find it—is an understanding of thought (or of knowledge) that is not reducible to the same space as that of the knowledge which is being investigated. Knowledge must, if genealogy is not to be self-refuting, stand on its own and be characterized in terms belonging solely to it. This is precisely what Deleuze provides with the concept of thought. And yet, even though he has introduced the concept, he has not shown how thought itself can be justified. How is it that thought reopens an epistemic space—a space without foundations to be sure, but epistemic nevertheless—that allows genealogy to be more than another expression of what it analyzes? How is thought to justify itself, so that its discoveries can be accepted as true (at least pending further inquiry) and not merely as a fable, entertaining but useless? Deleuze has succeeded in stating the issue, in citing its exact spot, and in demonstrating its epistemological nature; he has not, however, succeeded in resolving it.[1]

The issue is one of epistemic space. What Foucault needs in order to make his genealogy as compelling epistemologically as it is politically is a way to conceive of knowledge without any ultimate founding truths. He

1. Tom Keenan (1987) tried to resolve this Foucauldian impasse in another direction. He gave Foucault a Derridean reading which saw Foucault's terms as tracing an ambivalent movement in which they negated themselves as part of their articulation. Although a treatment of this interesting reading would lead us too far afield, it is worth noting that it also does not open up an epistemic space for its own justification. It seems, rather, to preclude such an opening by totalizing all epistemic space under the auspices of the currently dominant (in this case, political) positions.

needs to be able to provide a picture of knowledge that allows his genealogy to be convincing without its having to appeal to truths which are true beyond all dispute. In the absence of an alternative foundationalist schema, and with a political critique of much of our most precious knowledge as its goal, the genealogical project, in order to be able to justify itself, must show that knowledge can be conceived on a model that lacks the founding truths to which we are used to appealing in our attempts to justify knowledge. We must be able to conceive of justification without foundations.

The foundationalist schema of knowledge holds that justification comes to an end when it arrives at a truth that cannot be doubted. Justification, it will be recalled, has two aspects: the inferential move itself and the status of the claim to which the inferential move appeals in its attempt at justification. The first aspect is logical, comprising general deductive laws and inductive procedures; it asks the question, Would the justifying claim (or claims), if true, provide evidence to support the claim (or claims) that requires justification? For instance, does the rise of the asylum—if, indeed, there was a rise of the asylum—support the claim that madness was excluded from social discourse? This aspect of justification was never questioned by Foucault. In fact, his histories depend on it; and his methodological comments, in the first volume of *The History of Sexuality*, that further historical inquiry is needed in order to demonstrate or reject the repressive hypothesis testify to his commitment to this first aspect of justification. In order for historical inquiry to be able to demonstrate or reject anything, there needs to be a connection between what is demonstrating and what is demonstrated: there has to be a logical bond between the two. To question the general viability of the inferential move is to remove oneself from the possibility of argumentation altogether. What could be offered as evidence for or against such questioning that would not already require a bond between the evidence and the questioning itself?

It is the second aspect of justification, then, that distinguishes the foundationalist schema from Foucault's conception of knowledge: the status of the supporting claim. What all foundationalisms hold is that there are objectively certain claims, or that there is at least some sort of objectively certain epistemic space. Those claims or that space cannot be questioned; they are absolutely true. Moreover, foundationalism holds—as it must—that those claims or that space can constitute a sufficient ground for all our knowledge. In principle, all questions of knowledge can be settled by following the chain of justifications starting from the claim in question to see whether the last justification is one of the absolute claims or part of the absolute epistemic space. What the foundationalist schema requires, then, is an epistemic foundation that is both absolute and comprehensive.

In subjective foundationalism, that foundation is the mind. It is the mind to which all questions of knowledge are referred in order to see whether they conform to the strictures and constraints it presents. In the end, a claim is justified if it conforms to what the structure of the mind entails. An empirical claim, for instance, is justified if it is in conformity with the dictates of science, which are justified in turn because their rules of evidence are in conformity with the constraints and limits of what we can know, based on the fact that the human mind has this certain structure (it perceives thus, it thinks thus, etc.). This subjectivist schema is not unlike the traditional empiricist schema that sees knowledge as founded in sense-data (in fact, the only real difference, for our purposes, is in its holding the mind to constitute and not merely reflect sensory content), and the classic critique of that schema made by Wilfrid Sellars has relevance for all foundationalist schemas.

The traditional empiricist-foundationalist schema holds that all empirical knowledge (and thus all knowledge, since all knowledge is in the end empirically gained) is ultimately grounded in sense-data. Sense-data, those mute arrangements of color, tone, and so on which are the primordial sensory givens, are the last appeal for any empirical claim. If justification is to be had, then the sense-data will accord with either the claim or its implications; if not, then the claim is not justified. What Sellars shows is that this line of reasoning, which assumes there is something that can be noninferentially known (i.e., known foundationally and not on the basis of something else) leads to a trilemma:

A. X *senses red sense content s* entails *x non-inferentially knows that s is red.*
B. The ability to sense sense contents is unacquired.
C. The ability to know facts of the form *x is θ* is acquired.
   A and B together entail not-C; B and C entail not-A; A and C entail not-B. (Sellars 1963, p. 132)

What A states is that to sense a sense-datum or sense-content is a form of knowledge, a form which is foundational. What B states is that the sensing of sense-data is not an acquired ability, and therefore not something which can be mistaken. What C states is that to know something is to hold a claim, an ability which is acquired. The trilemma itself is this: if foundational knowledge of the sense-data sort is both knowledge and unacquired, then one can make claims without knowing language; if one must know language to make claims and if sensing sense-data is innate, then there is no foundational knowledge of the sense-data sort; if there is a foundational sense-data knowledge and if knowledge itself is an acquired ability, then sense-data knowledge cannot be innate.

The confusion here is a fundamental one for foundationalist empiricism, and it has to do with the nature of justification. What justifies a claim is not an experience but another claim. This follows from the first aspect of justification, that of the logic of inference. When one justifies a claim (or a group of claims), what one is doing is giving reasons for what one is holding to be true. To offer a mute experience of some sort in order to justify a claim is to offer an irrelevance: it is not mute experience which justifies a claim, but a claim about that mute experience, an interpretation of it. (It is also questionable whether one can even make sense of the idea of mute experience, as Derrida has shown. However, the weaker argument is enough to make our point.) One infers from claims to other claims, because inference—and, thus, justification—is something that happens within language, not outside it. To think there is a level of sense-data that, while not itself subject to justification, serves to justify all other empirical knowledge is to engage in what Sellars (1963, p. 140) calls "The Myth of the Given."

"The essential point is that in characterizing an episode or a state as that of *knowing*, we are not giving an empirical description of that episode or state; we are placing it in the logical space of reasons, of justifying and being able to justify what one says" (Sellars 1963, p. 169). When a claim is said to be known by someone, what we mean is that the person who knows that claim is capable of offering reasons for it which are accepted as valid inferential moves by the society or community in which that person lives. It does not mean that the claim is founded upon a sensory experience which renders it true in some indubitable fashion. Nor does it mean that it is impossible that what one seemed to know could turn out to be false. (But that falsity, too, would only be known on the basis of reasons.)

To know something is not to have a brute relationship with objective certainty; it is to be able to give acceptable reasons for what one believes.

It may be objected here that even if knowledge has to do with reasons, the last reason—the last claim to which one appeals—could be in some special relationship with reality such that it is in fact indubitable. But this is to misunderstand the linguistic nature of reasons and claims. To make a claim is to participate in a language, to engage in a social structure that one has acquired over time. And how one understands language is not, as Saussure and Sellars both show, to have a special relationship with reality such that one picks out terms of a language and applies them piecemeal to the world. For Sellars, this would be question-begging: what would the categories of the world be such that they correspond to the language one learns, but in a prelinguistic fashion? To have categories is to be in a language; it is futile to try to derive them from the world as though there were some remarkable coincidence between world and language that we could understand if only we were able get outside of language to see it (Sellars 1963, pp. 161–64). For Saussure (1959), too, the account of language occurs not in its relationship to a world that transcends it, but in the differences that arise within it. Meaning is not a product of word–world relationships, but of word–word relationships; thus, the claims made within language—and what else could be a claim?—cannot be reduced to a reflection of some brute reality that lies outside of language.

The argument Sellars offers is relevant not only to the schema of empiricist foundationalism, but to all foundationalism. If anything is to serve as a foundation of knowledge, it must be a claim or a set of claims that can be taken to be indubitable. But in what would this indubitability consist? It cannot be in a relation between language and the world that transcends it. Therefore, it must lie either in the compelling status of the claim itself or in a compelling status which derives from the relation of that claim to some other ones. What else could this compelling status be, however, other than the fact that one can come up with no good reasons to question it, that it withstands all scrutiny offered so far (since no one can tell what kinds of scrutiny will emerge in the future)? What makes a claim compelling is not a privileged relationship to something outside of justification, outside the space of reasons, but justification itself. A compelling claim is not one that is beyond justification, but one that is justified against all the arguments one might marshal against it.

The distinction being drawn here, one which has been slowly emerging throughout the present book, is that between justification and truth. Truth, as we have defined it, is a matter of "the way things are." As such, it has very little to do with knowledge, which is a matter of giving reasons. What knowledge seeks, of course, is truth (political motivations aside). But what serves to justify knowledge is not truth but claims that are taken to be true, either for the purposes of argument or beyond a specific argument itself. And those claims are taken to be true not because they are in fact true (although it may be that they are in fact true), but because they are justified by other claims. The picture of knowledge that emerges when one understands that it is justification and not truth which grounds it is not one of a hierarchy of claims founded on a bedrock of truth, but one of a network— or, better, a series of networks—of claims that are mutually reinforcing— both epistemically and semantically—and that are accepted as a whole in defining the parameters of knowledge. It is not that nothing in the world outside of language can influence knowledge, that knowledge is somehow immune from experience. In fact, many different things influence knowledge (a fact not often considered by those who would found knowledge on truth and, in turn, found truth on a single relationship, traditionally called a "correspondence with reality"). It is instead that experience does not determine knowledge; experience must be rendered linguistically before it can be relevant epistemically.

Truth, then, is not the measure of knowledge—justification is. This is the mistake shared both by the foundationalists and by the relativists, who differ not in their view of truth as providing the parameters of epistemology, but in whether to ratify epistemology on the basis of that view. Foundationalism, ignoring justification, seeks a truth that answers to no tribunal; relativism, equally ignoring it, seeks paradoxically a truth that will subvert truth. What foundationalism does not understand is that no claim is immune from question or doubt; the strength of a claim lies not in its indubitability but in its ability to respond to doubt. What relativism does not understand is that to refuse knowledge is as much an epistemic enterprise as to posit it; one does not escape epistemology by denial, one only makes oneself the object of one's questions.

But doesn't this picture of knowledge as justification subvert not only Foucault's relativism but his genealogical project altogether? For if knowledge is an epistemic matter, if it is a matter of justification, then what could politics have to do with it? Doesn't politics fall away by the same gesture with which brute sensory experience falls? No, because the genealogical critique holds whether or not a given area of knowledge can be epistemically justified. It must be recalled that what genealogy questions is not the epistemic standing of knowledge but its emergence and its links with various practices. This is not to accuse genealogy's object directly of being false or epistemically unjustified, but instead to accuse it of being oppressive. For genealogy, the traditional question of the epistemological status of its object is simply irrelevant. As Foucault put it, "It is not in the name of a political practice that one can judge the scientific quality of a science (unless the latter claims to be, in one way or another, a theory of politics). But in the name of a political practice one can question the mode of existence and the functioning of a science" (Foucault 1972c, p. 244).

But what of the suspicions genealogy raises about subjective foundationalism? Are not those suspicions epistemic as well as political, and thus open to the same objections that sense-data face? Here again, the answer is no, at least not directly. The suspicions raised against subjective foundationalism are not suspicions about whether psychological knowledge is epistemic as well as political. That would be to assume an identity between politics and knowledge which Foucault (at most times) is at pains not to do. What the genealogy of psychology puts into question is whether what is presented as an epistemic matter is indeed solely epistemic at all. The question is whether psychological knowledge, and all talk of the mind and subjectivity, is not ideological as well as epistemic. And to raise this suspicion, though without being able to resolve it (because genealogy is not capable of resolving the epistemic status of its objects), is not to contradict the "bracketing" of epistemic status which is one of the initial steps of genealogical method. Such suspicions, by showing the political embeddedness of the terms in which the debate has arisen, imply the impossibility of achieving the kind of neutral space desired by those who want to resolve the debate in the terms in which it has been cast.

Returning to the picture of knowledge as justification, we do not immediately see how debate might be resolved within the parameters such a picture lays out. It was stated that instead of seeing knowledge as a hierarchy based on a foundation of truth, knowledge should be conceived of as a series of networks of claims (or sets of claims) justifying one another in a sort of loose, ununified whole. This leaves it unclear, however, whether the totality of these networks is to be accepted as true, in which case one wonders how epistemic questioning could ever begin. Alternatively, if this totality is not to be accepted as true, then what kind of ground could it provide for claims that require justification? The question here has to do with our relationships to, and the relationships among and between, the networks of claims to which justification appeals. How can we conceive of these networks such that they are able to provide the ground which justification requires without becoming a self-sustaining foundation of circular reference?

The first step is to consider these networks of claims that provide justification not as a unified body of indubitable truth but, rather, as a background picture of how the world is, against which we compare claims and theories arising from our continuing experience. This background picture is not one that arises *ex nihilo* or from a scientific study of the world. Rather, it is the horizon of propositions within which the world comes to have meaning such that we are able to ask questions of it. In his remarks on certainty and doubt, Wittgenstein put it this way: "I did not get my picture of the world by satisfying myself of its correctness; nor do I have it because I am satisfied of its correctness. No: it is the inherited background against which I distinguish between true and false" (Wittgenstein 1969, p. 15e).

When a question or doubt arises, it is against this inherited background picture of how things are that it does so, a picture which in our society includes such claims as that people have minds and that minds have certain structures which it is the project of psychology to understand. To think of this background picture as one of uniform epistemic status—all claims in it being either true or false, equally justified or unjustified—is unwarranted, however. In fact, in any given picture of the world, some claims or theories are given up more easily than others. For instance, the claim that there is a process of evolution among organic beings is one that, in our culture, enjoys (probably unfortunately) a less integral status than other claims. There are discourses which, if their own inferential structure is to be accepted, throw doubt upon the justifiability of the claim of evolution. Other claims, though, are more integral and thus harder to remove from the background picture without throwing the whole picture into doubt. The example Wittgenstein offers (1969, p. 64e) is that of one's name. For one to doubt one's own name is to doubt one of the bases upon which one offers evidence for almost anything else. To be uncertain about one's own name is to be uncertain about one's memory and one's ability to comprehend things in such a radical way that one must wonder what one could accept in that situation which would provide evidence determining whether, indeed, one was right about one's name. The claim that one's name is so-and-so, then, is only barely a matter of knowledge, although it does form a part of one's background picture of the world. It is barely knowledge because there is very little one could accept as a justification for it that would not become doubtful with the same stroke by which one's name became doubtful; although one could imagine unusual situations in which doubt about one's name would make sense.

Thus, the series of networks of justifying claims, the inherited background picture of the world that one starts one's questions and doubts from, is not stable or uniform. It changes with one's life and it changes with history. Moreover, some claims within these networks are more rigid than others; when doubt arises, they are more likely to remain untouched, while claims around them are changed in order to keep them intact (although this does not mean that these claims, too, are immune from change). Indeed: "It might be imagined that some propositions, of the form of empirical propositions, were hardened and functioned as channels for such empirical propositions as were not hardened but fluid; and that this relation altered with time, in that fluid propositions hardened, and hard ones became fluid" (Wittgenstein 1969, p. 15e).

This reveals an important feature of justification attaching to specific claims within specific networks of discourse. It was shown above that claims have a twofold relationship to the network of which they form a part. First, as linguistic units, their meaning is dependent upon the place they possess within that network (as that network is dependent in a general way on the structure of language as a whole).[2] Second, as epistemic units, they are related in more or less integral fashion to other claims in the network of which they form a part. Since claims as epistemic units play the part (to a greater or lesser extent) of hinges—i.e., of allowing one to move from one claim to another by way of justification—then claims themselves, within the context of specific discourses or networks of claims, have an inferential role similar to that of the general logic of inference which runs through all discourse. Specific networks of claims, specific discourses, have their own types of inferential structure which depends upon the relationship among the claims within that network; inferential structure is not reducible to general laws of logic.[3]

That is why Foucault says, "The main problem when people try to rationalise something is not to investigate whether or not they conform to principles of rationality, but to discover which kind of rationality they are using" (Foucault 1981, p. 226; see Chapter 1, above). To focus on specific rationalities is not to reject reason, because all rationalities are governed by general logical laws. Rather, it is to recognize that claims within a specific discourse (what Wittgenstein called a "language-game") have their own inferential roles which are specific to that discourse, and that to question the rationality of that discourse is not to reject reason. "[T]he blackmail which has often been at work in every critique of reason or every critical inquiry into the history of rationality (either you accept rationality or you fall prey to the irrational) operates as though a rational critique of rationality were impossible" (Foucault 1983b, p. 201).

2. For an interesting treatment of the concept of linguistic meaning confluent with the picture of knowledge that is being elucidated here, see Lance and Hawthorne 1990.
3. Hence the importance of what has been called "material inference" in addition to the formal inferences of logic (cf. Sellars 1980).

Inference and justification, then, are not part of an indubitable web of truth. Instead, they are part of an imbrication of distinct networks of claims, each with its own rationality or inferential structure. That is why questions and doubts about our knowledge are possible, and why it is not possible to question or doubt it all at once. All doubting or questioning, if it is not to be a bare challenge ("How can you be sure?"), presupposes that there is something on the basis of which it has arisen. One questions the concept of the soul as a transcendental given on the basis of historical facts that lead one to be (politically) skeptical about it. One does not question those facts at the same time that one questions the soul; one holds those facts to be true, and on their basis one begins to wonder whether it makes sense to conceive of the soul as outside the forces of history and the processes of domination. One questions the concept of sexuality as the truth of human subjectivity on the basis of the history of sexual discourse, a history that one holds true while one puts sexuality as truth up for debate. "[T]he *questions* that we raise and our *doubts* depend on the fact that some propositions are exempt from doubt, are as it were like hinges on which those turn" (Wittgenstein 1969, p. 44e).

But why can't we just doubt everything, just issue a bare challenge to our knowledge? Because to do so would remove any possibility of answering the doubt. The only resources our knowledge contains in order to resolve questions of truth are the claims that are held true and that act as justifications for the answers given to those questions. To remove all possibility of justification reduces knowledge to pure decisionism, which is to say that it is no longer knowledge. In order to be able to say that one has answered a question or a doubt, one must be able to give evidence for that answer. A bare challenge to all knowledge removes all possibility of answer and, as well, all reason for doubting (on what basis would the doubt arise?); thus, doubting or questioning makes sense only in specific regions of knowledge.

For the same reason, questions must come to an end somewhere, and not necessarily at a point where questions are no longer logically possible. Foundationalism wanted the end of questioning to be a place of objective certainty, a place where it no longer made sense to raise questions. In fact, the end of questioning occurs not when it no longer makes sense to raise questions, but when the answers one gives seem so fundamental that one does not know how to give evidence for them. These are the "hardened propositions" of which Wittgenstein spoke. They form the hinges upon which doubt turns; to remove them is not to remove all doubt, but to force the structure they keep in place to collapse. The debate regarding abortion provides a good example of this. One of the places where questioning ends is when opponents of abortion claim that the fetus is a human being, no different from a child or an adult. Debate ends here not because the status of the fetus is an established fact in our society—far from it. Rather, to ask an opponent of abortion for evidence about why a fetus is really a human being is like asking him or her for evidence about his or her name; there is nothing that would count as evidence (Scripture excluded) that would itself be less doubtful to them than what that evidence would be trying to support. The status of a fetus as a human being is fundamental, not because doubt is logically excluded, but because of the place that belief has in the network of beliefs about abortion. "If I have exhausted the justifications I have reached bedrock, and my spade is turned. Then I am inclined to say: 'This is simply what I do' " (Wittgenstein 1958, p. 85e).

But if all doubt comes to an end, not in a place of objective certainty but in a place of pure conviction, then no claim is logically immune from doubt. There may be much of which I can say, "I wouldn't know how to go about answering doubts about that," but nothing of which I can say, "Doubt about that cannot even be conceived." Doubting or questioning even what seems most implausible to doubt can occur, given the proper background of claims held true. History offers many examples of this, of which Ptolemaic theory and the divine right of kings are two. And it is not only the evolution of history that can create such doubt; Einstein's theory of relativity is an example of what happens to knowledge when that which is indubitably true and that which is doubtful on its basis change places. If it is impossible to doubt or question everything at the same time, this is as much because it makes perfect sense to question anything as because it makes no sense to question everything. If the epistemic crux of knowledge lies in justification, then just as all doubt must have a background in order to resolve it, any part of that background can be brought forward for questioning in its own turn. "[E]mpirical knowledge, like its sophisticated extension, science, is rational, not because it has a *foundation* but because it is a self-correcting enterprise which can put *any* claim in jeopardy, though not *all* at once" (Sellars 1963, p. 170).

This picture of knowledge, in contrast to the foundationalist schema, makes it clear how Foucault's genealogical project can operate without falling prey to its own critiques. It is not, as Foucault himself sometimes thought, that the ground of genealogy lies in the ideological nature of knowledge. And it is not that there is nothing to say about the epistemological ground of genealogy. Rather, by recognizing that knowledge is a matter of justification, and that justification is a matter of the inferential structures of overlapping but distinct networks of claims or discourses, the epistemological aspect of genealogy becomes clear. Genealogy subverts the attachment to certain claims or sets of claims that have important inferential roles in a variety of discourses. It does so on the grounds of other claims or sets of claims that it holds constant. And what could be more important in its inferential role than a concept or a claim which functions as a foundation of much of our justification? When Foucault shows that the concepts of the soul, of modern sexuality, and of subjectivity, along with the claims that attach to those concepts, have a history—and an ignoble one at that—he raises profound questions about our knowledge, but on the basis of a historical record whose veracity remains untouched by the questions raised.

That is why genealogy's struggle against "the idea of universal necessities in human existence" is and must remain a local and epistemically restrained one. Genealogy is unavoidably micropolitical. For to deny those necessities generally is to engage in a transcendental argument that one wants to avoid; no amount of historical research will show that there are no such universal necessities. And to deny them epistemic value is to engage them at the site of the discourse one is trying to subvert. The genealogical project is accomplished neither by recourse to transcendental argument nor by epistemic refusal; it is accomplished by recognizing what it means to say that something is known, and by playing off some things that are claimed to be known against others, not in order to deny the truth of those others but to raise questions about their political role (and only thereby to cast some aspersion on their truth). Genealogy can be called a radical political empirics, wresting transcendental concepts and claims from their comfortable position at the foundation of knowledge, inciting suspicion about whatever appears in the guise of nature or necessity, provoking distrust of the transhistorical and the eternal—all by a tracing of historical lineages, an analysis of emergence and descent, that requires nothing more than a belief in historical fact.

But couldn't the strategy in which genealogy engages be applied to genealogy itself? Couldn't a genealogy of history be given that would cast doubt upon what Foucault holds constant in the genealogical project? And doesn't that possibility subvert genealogy's claim to provide an adequate critique of its object knowledge? The answer is that it may be the case that a genealogy of another genealogy is possible; but the mere fact of its possibility is not enough to subvert genealogy's claim. Foucault does not claim that it is possible to offer a genealogy of psychology and that therefore psychology is suspect. He actually offers one, and the threat it poses to psychology is in part dependent on the historical success—i.e., the epistemic justifiability—of the genealogy. The same would be true of a genealogy of that genealogy.

Foucault's own genealogy would be threatened if it could be shown that there was something suspect in the network of claims which he had held constant. But that would have to be shown by a concrete analysis that was itself justifiable on the basis of some set of socially accepted, epistemic inferential structures. The mere fact that all these structures are matters of social acceptance rather than transcendental guarantees is not enough to subvert them. This is the lesson of Wittgenstein's reflections on doubt. What is required, then, if one is to cast doubt or aspersion on Foucault's genealogies, is work that is empirically convincing. The claim that doubt is possible does not make it actual or compelling. What would make such a claim compelling would be the concrete analysis one engaged in to justify one's doubt. A genealogy, as a radical empirics, is subverted only by another empirical investigation that withstands critique upon its own grounds.

But if genealogy is a radical empirics, if it takes no refuge in transcendental foundations of discourse, then how does it arrive at the continuities that persist throughout the breaks in genealogical histories? How is discipline to be characterized as following torture, if not by reference to a unity underlying the historical facts which brings those facts together into a single history? Without transcendental concepts, isn't it not only foundations but unity as well that is lost, so that history becomes impossible by virtue of a dispersion without limit? It seems that in order for the genealogical project to be carried through, it must ultimately replace the transcendental concepts it subverts with transcendental concepts of its own; else it will have no justification for saying that one form of practice—such as discipline—follows upon another which is wholly distinct from it—such as torture.

John Rajchman has responded to this concern by calling Foucault's histories "nominalist," and in two senses (see Chapter 1, above): they are histories of names and practices, rather than objects; and they are themselves nominalist, using names to create unities rather than discover them. It has already been shown that Foucault's histories are histories of names and practices: the epistemic status of the objects of the discourses which genealogy examines is neither affirmed nor denied in the course of genealogical histories. However, Foucault did not resolve the problem of unity or continuity in his own work. This is evident from his use of the body as a transcendental concept to bind the history of punishment across its discontinuous breaks (see Chapter 5, note 4). But how can we address the problem of continuity and avoid the charge of an arbitrariness in regard to the unifying name such a history gives to the discourses it examines? How can the history of punishment, since it encompasses a diversity of practices and since genealogy allows no recourse to a transcendental object or practice to bind them, really claim that it is a history of any one thing at all?

The first step in resolving this problem is to recognize that, in the antifoundationalist picture of knowledge, a word or a claim comes to have meaning by virtue of its place both in the language at large and in the various discourses in which it functions. There is no question here of "natural kinds" which correspond to the category that names them by some sort of miraculous connivance between world and language: a correspondence theory of meaning makes no sense here. Instead, there is a role which a word or a claim plays relative to the other roles in a loosely structured whole—or, better, a series of wholes, since discourses have their own inferential autonomy—that, in the end, is the only space in which meaning can arise.

The question facing Foucault is not one of how he can invoke the name of nominalism (which he in fact did: see Rajchman 1985, p. 73) to describe his histories without falling into arbitrariness, but how specific names in fact delineate historical continuities. Continuity is not established through a transcendental or prelinguistic unity which comes to be named by a term that comes after it; instead, it occurs as part of the roles which terms and claims take up in the structures of different discourses. To seek the unity of the human body over time is not to inquire after something wholly outside of language that, by accident or miracle, came to correspond to a concept in our language; rather, it is to ask what role or roles the term "human body" may play in various discourses, and to see how far back in history that role or those roles can reasonably be said to be meaningful or useful.

So it is with punishment. The question of the continuity of punishment is not a question of whether there is a transcendental unity beneath punishment which confers a real sense of continuity to that which is said to be continuous (thus, there is no need for a transcendental concept of the body); it is whether there can be any sense in saying that the same thing is happening when one disciplines someone as when one tortures someone. Foucault shows in his history of punishment that there can be. At one time, discipline and torture were two separate activities with very little communication between them. However, as discipline became more widespread and capitalism more entrenched, discipline gradually came to replace torture (and the less harsh forms of punishment that succeeded torture) as a way of dealing with illegality. And although Foucault shows that with the rise of discipline as a penal technique the juridical opposition between the legal and the illegal served to obscure the strategic opposition between the illegal and the delinquent (Foucault 1977a, p. 277), there is nevertheless a penal continuity of discipline with torture: both are ways of dealing with the fact of lawbreaking.

In Foucault's texts, continuities and discontinuities are woven together to form a history which, though recognizable as our history, makes us appear strange to ourselves. This is not because Foucault arbitrarily lumps together historical items that are in reality separate, but because he uses unities that are generally forgotten in order to raise questions about unities that are taken for granted as natural. And if he can do this, it is not because he has found what is really going on in our history, as opposed to what people mistakenly think is going on, but because what is really going on in history (the ultimate truth of history) is not what grounds historical knowledge. Instead, what grounds such knowledge is what can be justified within the limits that comprise the structure of historical discourse; and, within those limits, Foucault's histories stake their claim to being justifiable histories with political and epistemological effects.[4]

So Rajchman is correct to say that Foucault's histories confer names as well as study them (although his use of the term "nominalism" misleadingly suggests that those histories are part of a debate which they are in fact foreign to). But this is not because Foucault's histories are special. All histories, whether they understand themselves to be so or not, confer unities upon a variety of historical events through the use of terms which gain their unifying character not by some bond with the transcendental, but by their role in the project of historical inquiry. What makes Foucault's histories special in this regard is that they reveal the creative role played by all historical inquiry, by showing that what are taken to be natural or transcendental principles for thought—madness, sexuality, the mind, sickness, and subjectivity—have a history that cannot be reduced to the progressive unfolding of truth.

Foucault himself did not always understand this. He was not conversant with the epistemic grounds of his own discourse, and he did not always recognize that his genealogies are rooted in the functioning of language and knowledge rather than in an ineluctable relativism. And thus he was led to ask, and to try to answer, questions that had no place in an inquiry such as

---

4. One can in fact ask what sense it would make to talk about "what is really going on" in our history as something distinct from all the accounts we can justifiably give of those goings-on.

his: Is truth an absolute matter or a historically relative one? Does genealogy believe in the truth of its object or not? Are the discourses that form the object of genealogy fact or fiction? By understanding knowledge as a matter of justification, and justification as a matter of inferential networks, the futility of these questions becomes evident, as does the incoherence that attaches itself to Foucault's attempt to answer them. The response to foundationalism is not relativism, but the antifoundationalism articulated here. And to the question of epistemic grounds which stalked Foucault's discourse and preoccupied his critics, especially those among the Critical Theorists, the reply is neither to deny that grounds exist nor to construct the foundation that seems to be called for. It is to explain why the grounds that Foucault gives in his histories are neither more nor less than what reasonably can be asked for. Genealogy, like Wittgenstein's later philosophy, is a therapy. Its project is not to resolve the problems that have preoccupied thinkers for the past two millennia, but to cure us of the temptation to continue thinking in the terms those problems have come to present themselves in. Genealogy does not help us find the foundations for our thought, but instead helps cure us of the temptation to keep looking. [5]

Foucault himself, although at times his effort was groping, had the deepest grasp among his contemporaries of what knowledge consisted in. He was able to avoid many of the problems of his peers, whose analyses are often beset by a vitiating relativism, be it ethical or epistemological. As Sam Weber points out in his afterword to Lyotard's *Just Gaming*, Lyotard, in his attempt to offer an account of justice that will respond adequately to what he calls our "postmodern" situation, winds up repeating the same mistake against which his analyses are directed: offering a grand narrative. "By prescribing that no game, especially not that of prescription, should domi-nate the others, one is doing exactly what is simultaneously claimed is being avoided: one is dominating the other games in order to protect them from domination" (Lyotard and Thebaud 1985, p. 105). In fact, it could be

5. The epistemological picture offered here as grounds for the genealogy can also serve as a picture of Foucault's moral grounding. Nancy Fraser (1981), understanding Foucault's epistemolog-ical stance, criticizes him for lacking the moral framework to answer the question, "Why ought domination to be resisted?" (p. 283). If moral discourse is conceived of along the inferential lines outlined here, however, then Foucault does not need an alternative moral framework any more than he needs an alternative epistemic foundation; he questions some moral stances on the basis of others. To give a full defense of this position in its ethical casting would require another book. Still, a remark of Wittgenstein's is suggestive: "no reason can be given why you should act (or should have acted) *like this*, except that by doing so you bring about such and such a situation, which again has to be an aim you *accept*" (Wittgenstein 1980, p. 16e).

argued that Lyotard's *The Differend* is an attempt to respond to just such a problem.[6]

Deleuze, although a more complex thinker, is tempted by a similar relativism. In order to avoid the totalization of dominant discourses, he periodically takes refuge in the idea of "haecceities," metaphysical singularities that can be neither the subject of any discourse nor the object of any investigation (cf. Deleuze and Guattari 1987, pp. 260–65). The role that haecceities (and other posits like "difference" and "incorporeal events") play in Deleuze's thought is that of irrecuperables, of moments which are revolutionary in their irreducibility to the categories of constituted knowledge. However, the relativist question which confronts Deleuze, and to which he never provided an answer, is this: How is he able to posit and indeed to analyze such irrecuperables if indeed they are resistant to constituted articulation? What is the space from which he speaks that is outside our knowledge, and what reasons can he offer us to believe him if that space is indeed outside our knowledge, outside the space of our reasons?

This recurrent problem of contemporary French thought, of the thought that has been called "poststructuralist," is, if the analysis of knowledge offered here is correct, one of failing to distinguish adequately between justification and truth. What Lyotard, Deleuze, and Foucault are all after is a way to question constituted knowledge from a political vantage point. In constructing their questions, however, they run the temptation to deny knowledge altogether (although they do so in quite distinct ways). What the distinction between justification and truth offers them, as Foucault's genealogies demonstrate, is a way to focus upon justificatory practices, questioning some of them on the basis of others, while at the same time leaving the issue of truth to one side (perhaps, as suggested above, because it is an epistemologically unenlightening concept). Such a bracketing of truth and a focus upon justification allows for local rather than global analyses, analyses that can raise the relevant political doubts about certain areas of our constituted knowledge while still leaving enough epistemic space for the justification of one's own discourse.

In closing this chapter, it would be worth turning briefly from knowledge to power, to see whether this discussion of the epistemic grounds of genealogy has any bearing on Foucault's conception of power. In his treatment of

6. For an interpretation of Lyotard along this line, see Hendley 1991. It could, however, be asked of *The Differend* whether, in promoting a profusion of discourses in the way it does, it commits the opposite—but complementary—mistake of precluding altogether the possibility of an ethical evaluation of nonethical discourses, or, as he calls them, "genres."

power, Foucault (1978a, p. 82) distinguished what he offered, which he called an "analytics of power," from any "theory of power." A theory of power is concerned with the nature of power, with its essence. Thus, "[i]f one tries to erect a theory of power one will always be obliged to view it as emerging at a given place and time and hence to deduce it, to reconstruct its genesis" (Foucault 1980a, p. 199). With an analytics of power, on the other hand, one moves "toward a definition of the specific domain formed by relations of power, and toward a determination of the instruments that will make possible its analysis" (Foucault 1978a, p. 82). An analytics of power, then, is concerned not with the essence of power but with its functioning in a given situation in given ways. This, of course, implies that Foucault can at least offer a definition, if not an essence, of power, so that one will understand what it is that is functioning in the ways he analyzes. He does this in his afterword to Dreyfus and Rabinow's *Michel Foucault*:

> In itself the exercise of power is not violence; nor is it a consent which, implicitly, is renewable. It is a total structure of action brought to bear upon possible actions; it incites, it induces, it seduces, it makes easier or more difficult; in the extreme it constrains or forbids absolutely; it is nevertheless always a way of acting upon an acting subject or acting subjects by virtue of their acting or being capable of action. A set of actions upon other actions. (Dreyfus and Rabinow 1982, p. 220)

Power is a network of actions upon actions, or forces upon forces. It can occur in many ways, and the analysis Foucault offers is concerned specifically with one of the ways in which it occurs: as the positive, productive, micropolitical power of the past several centuries.

The micropolitical exercise of power is thus a historically situated one for Foucault, eclipsing the more overtly repressive type of power that was predominant during the time of monarchical sovereignty. This conception of the micropolitical as historically situated runs counter to Deleuze's analysis of it as essential and transhistorical, and yet it is more in keeping with Foucault's commitment to historicizing seemingly transcendental concepts. What, then, are the characteristics of this modern power that distinguish it from the power of the preclassical epoch? Foucault lists these characteristics in many places in his texts (e.g., 1977a, pp. 23–24; 1978a, p. 94; 1980a, pp. 96–102, 142). No two of these lists are exactly the same, but all of them point to five central characteristics: power comes from within social and other relationships, not (or not only) from the top of the political order or from any single source; it is positive and productive, not negative and prohibitive; it is mutually reinforcing with relations of knowledge; it is always strategically oriented in a way that is "intentional and nonsubjective" (Foucault 1978a, p. 94); and it implies resistance. We discussed the first three characteristics in Chapter 3, and they are certainly consonant with an antifoundationalist epistemology; the last one will be discussed in the next chapter. It is the fourth characteristic, however, that of an intentional but nonsubjective strategic orientation, that has been the most controversial of Foucault's theses on modern power.

Such a thesis seems inseparable from Foucault's considerations on power. If power were not oriented in such a way that relationships of domination emerged, then what would be the political point of studying it? In order for there to be domination, and thus a need for genealogy, it would seem that an oriented strategic unity is a necessary aspect of power. Moreover, this unity must also be outside anyone's control, since it involves people's subjectification, and to maintain a sort of conspiracy theory regarding the process of subjectification—that modern sexuality, delinquency, and the mind are the products of conscious decision—is hardly plausible as an account of this process. Yet, there is something disturbing about holding modern power to function in a strategically oriented way. It seems to imply that power somehow takes on an ability normally ascribed to people—that of constructing an orientation for things—and such an ability seems to reintroduce transcendence back into the concept of power. For if modern power is capable of an intentional self-orientation without anyone's help, if it can coordinate a dispersion of micropolitical practices on a larger scale, then isn't Foucault propounding an "invisible hand" (Walzer 1986, p. 57) conception of modern power? And can Foucault actually propound this type of functionalism while remaining the antitranscendental genealogist that his epistemic statements make him out to be?

The problem for Foucault is one that hinges on the movement from the micropolitical to the macropolitical, from the tactical to the strategic. It is one thing to say that the macropolitical organization of micropolitical events and power relations has tended in recent history toward the domination of certain groups. But that is not Foucault's position. His claim is that the macropolitical has not only *tended* toward that domination, it has *intended* it. There is much more than a coincidence of forces oriented in a certain direction; there is an attempt, implicit in the coincidence of those forces, to orient them in that direction. As Colin Gordon explains: "What is meant by a strategy of power is the interplay between one or more programmes/ technologies and an operational evaluation in terms of strategy: a logically hybrid (and sometimes elusive) function which integrates the production of effects with the utilisation of those effects" (Gordon 1980, p. 252). What distinguishes a strategy from a micropolitical power relation, notes Gordon, is both its larger scale and its "non-discursive rationality" (p. 251). The strategy is a silent orientation of power, but no less intentional for its being silent and beyond individual control or even, in most cases, recognition. Thus, the strategic is "the arena of the cynical, the promiscuous, the tacit, in virtue of its general logical capacity for the synthesis of the heterogeneous" (p. 251).

This cynicism, this mute logic, this synthesis of the heterogeneous is precisely the problem. To posit a movement behind the phenomena—one that can be ascribed to no one but that is nevertheless intentional and directed—is to engage in transcendental thinking at its most explicit. It is to reintroduce "the idea of universal necessities in human existence," only now located outside the arena of conscious human practice rather than within it. It is, in the words of one critic, to engage in "essentialism" (Wickham 1983, p. 468) at the heart of a historical analysis.

What is more, it is wholly unnecessary. The concept of a strategic unity as an intentional organization adds nothing to what Foucault delineates in his genealogies as confluences of practices which form an orientation of forces that is oppressive. What the concept of intentionality seems designed to add to the notion of an oppressive convergence of practices is the extra moral sanction that Gordon calls "the cynical." There is something more sinister about an integration of heterogeneous practices whose purpose is to dominate and oppress than there would be if such an integration were contingent, or accidental, or just something whose cause cannot be understood.

An oppressive or dominating orientation of practices, however, becomes no less oppressive just because it may be accidental or unaccounted for. Indeed, the force of Foucault's treatment of knowledge as a tool of power lies precisely in recognizing that, at least on the micropolitical level, the ways in which knowledge often turns out to serve power are not cynical but instead quite innocent. There is no reason for not carrying the micropolitical treatment over into the macropolitical analysis and claiming that there has been an orientation of power relationships at the macropolitical level whose effects have been dominating and oppressive and have served certain interests over and against others, without having to make the further indefensible transcendental claim that the orientation of those effects has been the product of some design. In this way, the macropolitical level can be seen as an accumulation of similar local tactics that give an appearance of a global strategy (Wickham 1983, p. 481), as a collocation of local practices so diverse that "[a]t least some of the effects of one local tactic can join up with effects of another tactic, thereby producing an effect contrary to the strategic intent behind either of the two tactics" (Bersani 1977, p. 5), or as a unity without any orientation whatsoever, depending on the historical situation. What accounts for the orientation is not a strategic design outside the grasp of acting beings, but the coincidence and confluence of specific local practices in their interplay with each other. This interplay often eludes the analysis of those within it, not because of an "invisible hand" behind the practices, but because of the sheer number, complexity, and often accidental and unintended features of the practices themselves.

To conceive of power thusly is to keep within the bounds of the antitranscendental orientation which is the project of genealogy. It is to understand that power, like knowledge, can be accounted for without recourse to metaphysical explanation. And it is to recognize that there may be much more under our control than the seeming self-evidences of the age would lead us to believe. The goal of this orientation is clear:

> that criticism is no longer going to be practiced in the search for formal structures with universal value, but rather as a historical investigation into the events that have led us to constitute ourselves and to recognize ourselves as subjects of what we are doing, thinking, saying. . . . It is not seeking to make possible a metaphysics that has finally become a science; it is seeking to give a new impetus, as far and wide as possible, to the undefined work of freedom. (Foucault 1984c, pp. 45–46)

7

RESISTANCE

Genealogy is the micropolitical science. If the functioning of power over the past several centuries is no longer exhausted in the exercise of sovereign or sovereign-style repression, if in order to understand contemporary domination we must look not only toward the state but toward the small practices of knowledge and of discipline, then genealogy is the study of nonsovereign operations of power in the present age. Such a study is necessarily micropolitical. It concentrates not upon the obvious power wielded by recognizable institutions and classes in clearly cynical ways, but upon the effects of practices of detail, practices with no ostensible interest in power but whose products comprise an array of power relationships. Those small, and at times overlapping, practices—practices of medicine, penology, and psychology among them—create new fields of power by constraining action, by joining power to forms of knowledge, by seeping into the social fabric and tracing lines of obedience. Power is no longer articulated solely along the axis of sovereignty, but also along the axes of normalization and subtle constraint. Thus, there are "these two limits, a right of sovereignty and a mechanism of discipline, which define, I believe, the arena in which power is exercised"

(Foucault 1980a, p. 106). It is within the domain of discipline, among its discourses and its practices, that genealogy finds its objects.

What genealogy attempts to do is to realign our political thought, so that it will catch up with our political reality. We live in a world governed by powers which are micropolitical, which do not so much repress our inherent desires as create them, be it through public media, education, psychological discourse, or other forms of interaction. To continue to see ourselves in traditional political terms is to refuse to recognize the changes that have infused our political world. Moreover, such a refusal permits those changes to operate without restraint, since it is only when we begin to see what is happening to us—and what is happening to constitute us—that we may ask the question of which among these changes we shall endorse and which we shall reject. Genealogy, as we have interpreted it here, is the epistemic tool that allows us access to our micropolitical world.

The objects of genealogy are invariably—or at least have been so far—infused with power relationships that are inseparable from epistemic discourses. On the micropolitical level, knowledge is as much a political weapon as the walls of confinement or the guns of the police. Knowledge creates understanding and self-understanding where there was none before; and understanding and self-understanding, both for their attainment and as their consequence, constitute practices that set in place a series of constraints as effective as they are "natural"—flowing, seemingly, from the exigencies of knowledge rather than the manipulations of power. Thus, micropolitics and knowledge are often of a piece, knowledge stemming from small practices of power and in turn creating new spaces and new constraints for power's operation in the very attempt to realize its own project. The constraints of knowledge are more effective, if more dispersed and less governable, than other constraints imposed by power, because of an ideology which proclaims the purity of knowledge, its distance from matters of power and dominion.

But if so much of knowledge is entwined with power, if domination exists so often at the very sites where we thought we could keep our distance from it, does this not mean that all knowledge is suspect, that we should withhold our assent from everything? And if so, is not the product of genealogy really a surrender in the guise of a critique? To answer this, it must be recalled that in order for genealogy to function, not all knowledge can be suspect at the same time. This does not mean that genealogy is immune to critique; the categories genealogy holds constant in any of its analyses can always be put up for investigation by another history in an attempt to show that it was not power but something else that was at work. What it does mean, though, is that criticism is always situated; one does not criticize something except in the name of something else to which one gives one's assent. And just because that something else can also be questioned does not mean that it will turn out to be oppressive or that it is necessarily to be rejected. "My point," Foucault once said, "is not that everything is bad, but that everything is dangerous, which is not exactly the same thing. If everything is dangerous, then we always have something to do. So my position leads not to apathy but to a hyper- and pessimistic activism" (Foucault 1984b, p. 343).

For everything to be dangerous implies that everything must be open to investigation. Not everything can be questioned at the same time, but anything can be questioned in its turn. There is much to be questioned. Genealogy has shown that power often appears where it is least expected, that it is born and matures in the realization of projects which do not even recognize it as one of their own. Among those projects, epistemic projects hold a prominent place. Does this mean that we are to reject any knowledge that proves to be enmeshed in relationships of power? No. To be in a relationship of power is not a mark of immediate rejection, but an invitation to a vigilant investigation. If all practices—discursive or nondiscursive, epistemic or otherwise—are dangerous, that is because power relationships are everywhere. The answer to the question of power is not its rejection, however, nor the rejection of practices and discourses that participate in it. "[R]elations of power are not something bad in themselves, from which one must free oneself. I don't believe there can be a society without relations of power, if you understand them as means by which individuals try to conduct, to determine the behavior of others" (Foucault, in Bernauer and Rasmussen 1988, p. 18). Rather, the answer is to study discourses and practices, to determine the nature and extent of the constraints they impose, and to evaluate whether those constraints are acceptable or not. If it is asked in what or whose name the determinations of acceptability are to be made, one can only answer that it depends upon the evaluator and the context of evaluation. There is no necessary stopping point for moral or political evaluation, as there is none for epistemic investigation. Agreement is always contingent upon the acceptance of some basic values (basic in the sense of allowing resolution); where those are lacking, discussion breaks down. It is the illusion of foundationalism—ethical this time—that there are values which necessarily close debate. To expect such closure is to be ignorant of the open-endedness of ethical and political discussion; to proclaim it is a police operation, not just a philosophical one.

The genealogical project, then, is a political critique of micropolitical practices. It is not against knowledge, for it is in the name of knowledge that the critique operates. It is not against practice; it is for the sake of practice that the critique is made. And the practice that is the for-the-sake-of-which of genealogical critique is resistance, a resistance whose contours and possibilities we must understand in order finally to grasp the genealogical project and the critique of psychology that is so much a part of it. To understand the nature of this resistance will be to recognize the general character of micropolitical intervention available to us in a world no longer governed solely by means of sovereign power.

For Foucault (1978a, p. 95), power implies resistance: "Where there is power, there is resistance, and yet, or rather consequently, this resistance is never in a position of exteriority in relation to power." As a constraint upon action, power is necessarily resisted because it is necessarily constraining. It is resisted not by a force external to it, but precisely at the point of its application. Power does not come to bear upon a material that is submissive to it or that it molds to the image of its orientation. Instead, power is one half of a two-pole relationship, power/resistance, in which force is always pitted against force, the constraining action against the action it is trying to constrain.

However, this picture of resistance, as Colin Gordon points out, implies that there is something either beneath or beyond power to which power applies and which has the character of being resistant. "The field of strategies is a field of conflicts: the human material operated on by programmes and technologies is inherently a *resistant* material" (Gordon 1980, p. 255). Such a picture raises a problem for Foucault. The idea of an inherently resistant material is a transcendental one; it posits something outside the arena of productive power as the transcendental substance upon which power operates. The notion of a transcendental substance which is the object of power runs against the grain of Foucault's thought, both in its essentialism and in contradicting his notion of power as positive and productive. The return to a transcendental substance beneath or beyond power is a return to the juridical model of power: power is a repressive force, denying expression to an otherwise liberated substance or being.

What Foucault wants to acknowledge with the concept of essential resistance is the permanent possibility of revolt. He wants to elicit the recognition that the contingencies of history by which we have achieved our present are precisely that—contingencies—which can be, and often are, struggled against and altered. Thus he finds resistance to be immanent to the power relationship, which makes every application of power a historical event and every constraining–constrained relationship a fragile balance. Like the refusal of truth, however, the refusal of an unresisted power is a transcendental one. It cannot be had without conceiving a substance beneath or beyond discourses and practices (such as, for instance, Foucault's concept of the body) which is the subject of refusal and the locus of revolt. Foucault does not need a transcendental substance to make the genealogical point. His histories—fragile, uncertain, changing at seemingly the most stable points, tracing the rise of "truths" which we thought were outside the vagaries of history—are all that genealogy requires in order to account for the possibility of resistance. Since Foucault does not want to prescribe for history what its nature is, he does not need to prescribe for the relationship of power what its essence is. He needs only to show where and how resistance to power has appeared in specific cases and with specific results.

It might be objected here that Foucault can make his case for power implying resistance without a turn to the transcendental. He can claim that since power is a constraint upon action, there is no need for power where actions do not need to be constrained. Thus resistance, rather than being part of the transcendental essence of power relationships, is merely part of their definition. Power exists only where action needs to be constrained and, thus, only where there will be resistance. In this way, there need be no material beneath or beyond power to which it is applied, only specific actions that can be cited as the objects of power's interventions. Psychological constraints upon human behavior try to ensure that behavior will follow only strictly designated paths and not those paths which it might otherwise follow if there were no such constraints.

This objection is surely closer to the spirit of Foucault's genealogical project than the concept of a resistant material. But power, as a constraint upon action, is applied not only to actions that are themselves resistant, but also to actions that can be but are not yet resistant. Psychological discourse and practice are relevant to human behavior not only because they quell resistance, but also (and more to the point) because they try to preclude it. Psychology impinges upon human action in order to trace out paths for it that, via the project of the soul's or the mind's self-understanding, prevent the realization or even the consideration of resistance in the course of one's behavior. Power does act upon concrete instances of resistance, it is true; but it also acts upon cases of possible resistance, by precluding them through the positive project of creating knowledge and action in accordance with its own principles of discipline, obedience, and a descending individualization.[1]

Resistance, then, is a contingent event, appearing not of necessity but just when it does in fact appear. And when it does appear, it is often, as Foucault has shown, a local and not a global resistance. This does not mean that there is no global resistance; resistance to sovereign forces of repression—a resistance that usually occurs in the name of some right—is a common and often justified struggle. What it means is that the struggle against domination is not reducible to resistance against the exercise of sovereign power. Foucault distinguishes between exploitation and domination through power: "systems of domination and circuits of exploitation certainly interact, intersect and support each other, but they do not coincide" (Foucault 1980a, p. 72). Exploitation, which is an economic category, is realized with the political interventions of the state, interventions that often involve repression and violence. However, domination through micropolitical systems of modern power occurs at a variety of sites and in a variety of ways, and the struggle against each domination is a struggle with its own integrity, irreducible to the Marxist struggle against exploitation. "[A]s soon as we struggle against exploitation, the proletariat not only leads the struggle but also defines its targets, its methods, and the places and instruments for confrontation. . . . But if the fight is directed against power, then all those on whom power is exercised to their detriment, all who find it intolerable, can begin the struggle on their own terrain and on the basis of their proper activity (or passivity)" (Foucault 1977b, p. 216).

Although heterogeneous from each other, the struggles against exploitation and micropolitical domination are bound by the fact that the exploitation and the domination they struggle against are mutually reinforcing. In *Discipline and Punish*, Foucault remarks:

> If the economic take-off of the West began with the techniques that made possible the accumulation of capital, it might perhaps be said that the methods for administering the accumulation of men made possible a political take-off in relation to the traditional, ritual, costly, violent forms of power. . . . [I]t would not have been possible to solve the problem of the accumulation of men without the growth of an apparatus of production capable of both sustaining them and using

1. This notion of human behavior should not be mistaken for another transcendental material. By "human behavior" is meant nothing more than the fact that human beings act. Thus, psychology's application to human beings is not a repression but, rather, a creation.

them; conversely, the techniques that made the cumulative multiplicity of men useful accelerated the accumulation of capital. (Foucault 1977a, pp. 220–21)

But at the level of power, at the level of the realization of the capitalist project through forms of constraint, the micropolitical has a certain primacy in two senses. First, the creation of the docile and maximally effective worker who is crucial for the smooth functioning of capitalism is a disciplinary project: "the body becomes a useful force only if it is both a productive body and a subjected body" (Foucault 1977a, p. 26). Second, the state which ensures the continuation of capitalism on the political level is dependent for its own functioning on the disciplinary strategies that lie at the micropolitical level. Earlier it was noted that Foucault was able to abide the notion of state power alongside that of micropolitical practices. This remains true. However, state and micropolitical power are more intimate in their relationships than the heterogeneity of the registers of their functioning might lead one to believe. Thus: "I do not mean in any way to minimise the importance and effectiveness of State power. I simply feel that the excessive insistence on its playing an exclusive role leads to the risk of overlooking all the mechanisms and effects of power which don't pass directly via the State apparatus, yet often sustain the state more effectively than its own institutions, enlarging and maximising its effectiveness" (Foucault 1980a, pp. 72–73).

This is why Foucault emphasizes the integrity and irreducibility of local struggles. Marxists have accused him of neglecting the role of state repression and state violence in his considerations of power (Poulantzas 1978, p. 78) and of supporting a regionalism that does not block, but instead reinforces, bourgeois fragmentation (Comay 1986, p. 118). However, Foucault's concern—and it is a concern which has its roots in recent history—is that a change in the state apparatus which does not address micropolitical forms of domination runs the risk of merely allowing power to change hands rather than altering its structure. To centralize economic relationships or to abolish the private extraction of surplus value without recognizing that domination is not reducible to exploitation is not to break from the oppression of capitalism, but to invite a continuation in the new society of all the forms of domination that were inherent in the old one. "One can say to many socialisms, real or dreamt: Between the analysis of power in the bourgeois state and the idea of its future withering away, there is a missing term: the analysis, criticism, destruction, and overthrow of the power mechanism itself" (Foucault 1976b, p. 459).

The risk of a totalizing theory of politics is that it will unsuspectingly promote what it struggles against, because it is ignorant of oppressions at the micropolitical level. The alternative to this, though, is not a bourgeois reformism but what one critic has called a "radical reformism" (Gandal 1986, p. 122). This radical reformism recognizes both that a change of power which comes solely at the top hazards a repetition of the old forms of domination and that not just any small reform will change micropolitical domination. Instead, what the radical reformist seeks are changes at the micropolitical level which actually change the relations of power between groups. Those changes involve very different types of struggle, depending upon the situation of the groups involved. They cannot be cast in a common form or be reduced to a common goal. But they possess a solidarity that derives from a complementarity investing all struggles against domination under capitalism.

Micropolitical struggles do not replace the struggle against exploitation, and no one of them can be substituted for the others. What binds them is the recognition that in the modern epoch power operates in many and diffuse ways, and that to end the domination of such power is a matter of many independent but mutually reinforcing struggles both at the micro-political and the macropolitical level. And thus, there is a need for the kinds of analyses which are situated not in the region of general political theory, but in the domains of struggles which occur both beneath and across that region. "I am attempting . . . apart from any *totalization*—which would be at once *abstract* and *limiting*—to *open up* problems that are as *concrete* and *general* as possible, problems that approach politics from behind and cut across societies on the diagonal, problems that are at once constituents of our history and constituted by that history" (Foucault 1984b, pp. 375–76).

Resistance, at least that kind of resistance which arises in response to micropolitical domination, is articulated in the specific struggles from which it arises. That is why Foucault is so reticent to offer programs of action in the course of his genealogies. The task of the intellectual is no longer to pronounce the truth of the revolt against a power both sovereign and repressive; it is to analyze specific forms of domination and to participate alongside—not above—those who are resisting those forms. "The intellec-tual no longer has to play the role of an advisor. The project, tactics and goals to be adopted are a matter for those who do the fighting. What the intellectual can do is to provide instruments of analysis, and at present this is the historian's essential role. What's effectively needed is a ramified, penetrative perception of the present" (Foucault 1980a, p. 62). The genealogical project precludes the genealogist from dictating the nature of struggle and resistance; to do so would be both to pass judgment upon the truth of history and to decide for the oppressed what the nature of their struggle is to be. Instead, the genealogist documents oppression and domination, patiently detailing their emergence and descent, in order to be able to offer the oppressed one of a number of tools they will need in their struggle against the more insidious forms of modern domination.

If the project of the genealogist is not to detail specific programs of resistance, genealogy can at least offer, besides its analyses, some general theses about what micropolitical struggles look like. Although Foucault never listed these theses himself, there are four which emerge from a reading of his work; and these four theses center around a single concept: freedom. Freedom, for Foucault, is not a metaphysical or a transcendental concept. It is not opposed to determinism, and it does not affirm some reserve within the human subject that is capable of breaking the bondage of micropolitical domination. It is instead a pedestrian concept. Free subjects are those "who are faced with a field of possibilities in which several ways of behaving, several reactions and diverse comportments may be realized" (Foucault, in Dreyfus and Rabinow 1982, p. 221). In other words, freedom is the open-endedness and contingency of the constraints imposed by power. To make freedom a project is not to peel away any metaphysical or political coverings in order to reveal a nascent or oppressed subjectivity. It is to engage in "a diagnosis of the present" which tries to "open up a space of freedom understood as a space of concrete freedom, i.e., of possible transformation" (Foucault, 1983b, p. 206). Freedom is a concrete project of change from specific forms of domination to alternative courses of behaving and acting in which the relationships of power are more tolerable.

This freedom is the basis for Foucault's four theses concerning resistance. The first is that freedom is not a matter of liberation. There is no reason to posit a transcendental subjectivity, an alienated human nature, or a distorted arena of pure communication which it is the project of political theory and practice to rescue. To seek the subject of liberation is to misunderstand the functioning of modern power. It is to conceive power on the basis of the classical juridical model of repression. This juridical model, which was a viable description of the functioning of power during the predominance of monarchical sovereignty, acts now less as a vehicle for understanding the functioning of power than as a mask for concealing its positive, productive aspects. No longer can we understand power merely in terms of the negative and uniform functions of rule, prohibition, censorship, and law (Foucault

1978a, pp. 82–84); ironically, it must be approached as the author of that which is too often conceived as the means of liberation from it—subjectivity, soul, sexuality, health. But if micropolitical power does not operate by means of repression, then its transformation cannot operate by means of liberation. Instead of the concept of liberation, Foucault offers the terms of war and strategy as the way to engage in micropolitical struggle. It is not a matter of seeking the truth that makes one free (genealogical history has abolished the immediate identification of knowledge and freedom), but a matter of recognizing the values to be struggled for—and against—in a situation where friend and enemy, collaboration and resistance, are no longer taken for granted but are enmeshed in a complex of relations often difficult to disentangle.

And thus the second thesis on freedom: freedom is not a matter of "universal necessities of human existence," but one of concrete struggles for situated values. The entire orientation of genealogy is opposed to the idea that there is something eternal in the human situation which it is the project of political struggle to realize. Genealogy's historicization of values and concepts which present themselves as beyond the pale of human intervention is intended to show that no value can be held without question as founding for the spectrum of political action. For Foucault, the "recourse to history— one of the great facts in French philosophical thought for at least twenty years—is meaningful to the extent that history serves to show how that-which-is has not always been . . . and [how] the network of contingencies from which it emerges can be traced" (Foucault 1983b, p. 206). To engage in political action, to carve out a concrete space of transformation, is to confront some values with others, some knowledge-claims with others—not in the name of truth or eternity, but in the name of a concrete refusal of domination or a concrete and situated value to be realized. The thought that there could be a more universal foundation for resistance is itself a dangerous one. It tempts the resister into forming new institutions which promote new hierarchies for the sake of new final answers that, as the Soviet experience has shown, are more a repetition of old practices of domination than a liberation from them.

The third thesis on freedom is a corollary to the previous two: freedom is a matter of historical contingency. It is not inscribed in the course of history that any given concrete change is necessary. Because change comes from a network of intersecting and often unrelated practices, because accidents or chance can change the course of events, the struggle for change is never assured of success. To claim that one is on the side of history is not only to display a dangerous adherence to transhistorical values; it betrays as well an ignorance of historical process. It must be understood that there are no givens in history—at least, none so far as we have been able to discern. This contingency means that the idea of being able to control events or to read their historical destiny must be abandoned in favor of trying to understand both the tactical and the macropolitical orientation of events, and this in order to fashion, to the best of one's ability, a strategically appropriate response.

The fourth thesis on freedom is that there is no necessary end point in the struggle for it; resistance may not have a Promised Land. This is not the same as saying that there is no destiny to history. It is instead the recognition that there may not—although there may—come a day of harmony, or even complementarity, of concrete spaces of freedom. Although there is a complementarity of struggles against the various oppressions of the capitalist epoch, it may be that intersections among them result in other situations of domination and conflict. These conflicts may not cease to arise: "One has to recognize the indefiniteness of the struggle—though this is not to say it won't some day have an end" (Foucault 1980a, p. 57). An inherent aspect of all resistance, then, must be a vigilance not only to the effects of what it struggles against, but to its own effects as well. Struggle can deny neither its own historical contingency nor the complexity of the historical process; if it cannot take a knowing responsibility for all its effects in advance, it can at least foster enough historical suspicion to be watchful of them as they unfold.

These are the broad parameters within which a resistance according to genealogical principles can be conceived. Beyond these principles, Foucault never articulated a positive program for concrete transformations except once, in the first volume of *The History of Sexuality* (1978a, p. 157), where he remarks that "[t]he rallying point for the counterattack against the deployment of sexuality ought not to be sex-desire, but bodies and pleasures." Although much criticized (e.g., Cousins and Hussain 1984, pp. 223–24), this remark can, and probably should, be seen as a suggestion that the discourse of oriental *ars erotica* be considered as an alternative to the Western discourse of *scientia sexualis* in approaching the domination of sexuality in our culture. More interesting than this remark, however, are the last of Foucault's writings, which, though not providing a program of resistance, articulate approaches to the formation of subjectivity in earlier cultures. These writings reveal not only that other forms of self-understanding are possible—and, more than possible, actual at one time—but also that the psychological understanding of subjectivity, dominant still in our culture, is only one of many styles of self-formation open to people with our history.

It is not surprising that psychology would figure prominently in Foucault's last writings, since it was an abiding theme throughout his previous investigations. What is remarkable about these writings, however, is that, while directly relevant to the problem of psychological discourse and practice, psychology is neither mentioned nor treated in them.[2] In the genealogical works, Foucault's criticism of psychology took the form of a tracing of the descent and emergence of psychological discourse and practice. In the last writings, those which Foucault called "ethical," the critique of psychology takes a different, altogether oblique, path. Instead of showing how it is that psychology was crucial to the formation of contemporary subjectivity, Foucault shows that it is possible to have a coherent subjectivity without the interventions of psychological practice.

This does not mean that Foucault endorsed the subjectivity—or, better, the "technology of the self" (Foucault 1984b, p. 342)—that he found in the Greeks (or later, differently wrought, in the Romans and early Christians). He didn't.[3] But by returning to the ancient Greek activity of self-formation, particularly ethical self-formation, Foucault was able to accomplish two tasks that were outside the scope of his previous writings. First, he was able (or would have been able) to offer a genealogy of the modern subject in a way that was more complete than any of his previous writings, by virtue of investigating a longer historical span. Here the roots of psychology could have been discovered in discourses and practices both older and more diffuse than studies starting with the preclassical epoch could recognize. More important, however, he was able to tear us from the seeming naturalness of our own, largely psychological, sense of subjectivity by presenting a technology of the self which was different, yet still belonged to us.

The final goal of Foucault's last investigations was laid out in his introduction to the second volume of *The History of Sexuality*, *The Use of Pleasure* (in French, *L'Usage des plaisirs*):

> As for what motivated me, it is quite simple; I would hope that in the eyes of some people it might be sufficient in itself. It was curiosity—

2. These writings are treated only briefly here, both because their relationship to psychology is indirect and because the present book views the genealogical works as the centerpiece of Foucault's work, correcting the earlier texts and forming the foundation for the later ones.

3. In what is reportedly his last interview, Foucault had an exchange with his interlocuters that went like this: "Q: . . . The Greeks—did you find them admirable? F: No. Q: Neither exemplary nor admirable? F: No. Q: What did you think of them? F: Not very much. . . . All of antiquity seems to me to have been a 'profound error' " (Foucault 1985a, p. 2).

the only kind of curiosity, in any case, that is worth acting upon with a degree of obstinacy: not the curiosity that seeks to assimilate what it is proper for one to know, but that which enables one to get free of oneself. After all, what would be the value of the passion for knowledge if it resulted only in a certain amount of knowledgeableness and not, in one way or another and to the extent possible, in the knower's straying afield of himself? (Foucault 1985b, p. 8)

To become someone else: that is the ultimate goal of the ethical writings. Not to become Greek, or Roman, or Christian; but, through creating a distance between whoever one has been taught that one is and who one could have been, to open up the possibility that one might become someone else. If we can appear strange to ourselves even in our own history, then perhaps we can fashion ourselves to become other than we are, creating of ourselves beings far different from anything we have ever imagined.

Deleuze (1988, p. 97) has called the process of subjectification a "fold of the outside." Rather than arising from a movement of interiority, subjectification is created by a movement in which the outside is folded back upon itself, forming a pocket that is called the subject: "[t]he inside as an operation of the outside" (p. 97). This is right. The subject arises not through the development of an interiority whose secret belongs wholly to itself, but through a process of self-formation that is inseparable from, indeed dependent upon, one's historical, social, and political situation. Self-formation, subjectification, is a process not of unfolding but of folding, the folding back upon itself of the outside which one always already is, and the escape from which involves not a return to the inside, but a different kind of folding.

The overcoming of psychology, then, occurs in a project that has nothing to do with interiority. It is not performed by a return to anything. Its first step is the recognition that the self is a historical construction, not a metaphysical one. One's subjectification occurs through an encrustation onto a history and a politics that are not the mystification of one's identity but the very substance of it. On the basis of that recognition, one can learn about what other processes one's subjectification is connected to (archaeology), about how it arose (genealogy), about the problematics that constitute it (ethics). And by tracing these lines of connection and intersection, by forming a concrete picture of who one is and how one came to be that way, one prepares oneself for a freedom that comes not by liberation, not by transcendental discovery, but by concrete transformation (or transformations) of who one is into who else one would like to be.

Summarizing Foucault's last works, John Rajchman wrote: "A 'modern practical philosophy' is therefore one which, instead of attempting to determine what we should do on the basis of what we essentially are, attempts, by analyzing who we have been constituted to be, to ask what we might become" (Rajchman 1986, p. 166). It is a practice of getting free of "universal necessities in human existence," not by finding other necessities but by understanding how we came to believe in the ones we did. It is a practice of overcoming the ways we have been taught to think about ourselves—ways that so often involve psychology—in order to engage in a different thought and a different experience. It is a practice of experimentation: the experimenting with new identities that comes along with both an understanding of how the old identities were created and a vigilance about unforeseen effects of the new ones.

What, then, is to become of psychology? Are we to experiment with new identities, or with no identities at all, and reject the identities offered us by psychology? In his works on the prison and sexuality, Foucault offers strong reasons to reject psychological thinking outright. Whereas in *Histoire de la folie* the motivation for abandoning psychology lay in its effect upon those considered to be mad, in the later works psychology is seen as subjecting—in both senses of the word—everyone in European society. All are constrained to participate in a process of identity formation which marks out certain relationships among and within people that will be accepted and cultivated, others that will be monitored, and still others that will be suppressed.

And yet, as a specific intellectual, Foucault would overstep his role in two ways were he to advocate a wholesale rejection of psychology and psychological identity. First, he would be prescribing for others a course of activity leading to their liberation, rather than providing a tool or a weapon that they may use. It is true that Foucault himself, as a member of European society, is also a subject of psychology. He may choose to reject psychology because of the constraints it presents. He may even join with others who feel the oppression of psychology in order to consider specific alternatives to it in their own lives. He cannot, however, prescribe the rejection of psychology to others in the way some intellectuals prescribe the overthrow of capitalist relations of production.

Second, Foucault's genealogies of psychology have not shown that psychology is in itself an oppressive force. Its oppressiveness has emerged in combination with the emergence and decline of other practices specific to European and European-influenced society. Psychology is oppressive to us today not because psychological thinking is necessarily evil, but because, in combination with contemporary medicine, advanced capitalist relations of production, religious practices, and so on, it creates and reinforces practices of self-formation that continue relations of domination and exploitation, and because it denies access to other possibilities of self-formation without adequate reason. It is conceivable, within the parameters of Foucault's work, that there are (or could be) societies in which psychology would not play an oppressive role. Those societies would be very different from our own. But that very conceivability indicates that it is not psychology which is at issue in formulating projects of resistance, but instead the place and role of psychology in contemporary society.

Resistance in contemporary society does not require the complete abandonment of psychology. What it does require is an understanding of the ways in which psychology has contributed to our present, particularly the dangers it poses and the damages it has fostered in that present. It is indeed important for us to get free of psychology. But to get free of psychology is not necessarily to abandon it. It is to understand its hold on us, theoretically and practically, and to be able to make choices about what place, if any, we want it to have in our future. If Foucault's last works on Greek and Roman sexuality were not written in order to offer concrete alternatives to contemporary methods of self-formation, neither is the idea of experimentation which motivated them an implicit advocacy of the complete abandonment of psychology. They are an attempt to understand who we are and what our present is like, by reference to histories of practices rather than to the unfolding of truths or falsehoods.

To get free of psychology and of the specific subjectification in which it is involved is not, of course, to be rid of power relationships. Rather, it is to abolish a certain set of power relationships, relationships whose effects we have good reason to find intolerable. It would be naive to think that, by abolishing the dominations inhering in psychological discourse and practice, power relationships will thereby be relegated to the past. If genealogy has taught us anything, it has taught us that the effects of our actions rarely run a straight line; they intersect with other effects in order to create situations that none of us could have imagined. Thus, the overcoming of psychology must occur not through a sweeping gesture of denial, but by an experimentation that is as "gray, meticulous, and patiently documentary" as genealogy itself. On the basis of what we have been constituted to be, we ask what we can become. And on the basis of what we try to become and who we do in fact become, we must ask again—and always—how we got there and what the effects, political and otherwise, of being there are.

And thus, in the end, the question of resistance, like the questions of knowledge and of power, is an inquiry to be posed to our present. Who we are, how we got here, and what we can do are Foucault's preoccupations, as they have been for thinkers over the course of our history; but, for Foucault, these issues are not a matter of an eternity that is distant to our situation, but precisely a matter of our situation itself. The critique of psychology, the political interrogation of subjectivity and sexuality, the genealogy of various foundations of our knowledge—these are arrows pointed not at the beyond but at who we are in the present moment. Perhaps above all, Foucault's work inspires a critical vigilance that branches out in several directions: toward who we are told we are, toward what we take for granted, toward the unintended consequences of what we do. "The critical ontology of ourselves has to be considered not, certainly, as a theory, a doctrine, nor even as a permanent body of knowledge that is accumulating; it has to be conceived as an attitude, an ethos, a philosophical life in which the critique of what we are is at the same time the historical analysis of the limits that are imposed on us and an experiment with the possibility of going beyond them" (Foucault 1984c, p. 50). We must recognize that our history is not given to us outside our own making of it and, yet, that history, though contingent, possesses a density which imposes itself upon all our actions. Recognizing this, we must commit ourselves to practices which seek to change that history in the multitude of oppressions it has burdened us with, while at the same time understanding that those practices, too, will be dense with effects we may not comprehend until they have betrayed us.

It is this recognition, and this attitude, that animated Foucault's thought from beginning to end. Michel de Certeau called it "the laugh of Michel Foucault," writing about his various periods that

> [t]hese successive places are not linked by the progress of an Idea that would gradually formulate itself, but by a common *way* of thinking. They answer to the laughs of history. They attest to the necessity of inscribing these chance happenings one after another in our domains of knowledge; they do not undertake, by homogenizing all the discourses, to return their dazzling discontinuities to the shadows. Rarely has philosophical astonishment been treated in a manner so mindful of its possible developments and respectful of its surprises. (Certeau 1986, p. 197)

Foucault leaves us not with the phosphorescences of a grand and futile gesture of desire, nor with the stilted realism of a bourgeois thought whose only passion is to preserve its own hegemony. He leaves us with a critical vigilance that is both an irony and an engagement. This vigilance is the animating force behind the critique of psychology; it is that which leads from archaeology to genealogy to ethics. And if, finally, Foucault fell prey to some of the transcendental demons it became his task to exorcise, if he was at moments captured by them from behind, this should lead us to realize once again the significance of his project: to free thought from densities both formidable and contingent in order that we may recognize, understand, and change our present in the ways and to the limits that the eventualities of our history permit.

REFERENCES

Allison, Henry. 1983. *Kant's Transcendental Idealism: An Interpretation and a Defense.* New Haven: Yale University Press.

Althusser, Louis, and Etienne Balibar. 1970. *Reading Capital* [1965], trans. Ben Brewster. New York: Avon Books.

Barthes, Roland. 1972. "Taking Sides" [1964]. In *Critical Essays*, trans. Richard Howard. Evanston: Northwestern University Press.

Baudrillard, Jean. 1987. *Forget Foucault* [1977], trans. Nicole Dufresne. New York: Semiotext(e).

Bernauer, James, and David Rasmussen. 1988. *The Final Foucault.* Cambridge: MIT Press.

Bersani, Leo. 1977. "The Subject of Power." *Diacritics* 7, pp. 2–21.

Brandom, Robert. 1988. "Pragmatism, Foundationalism, and Truth Talk." *Midwest Studies in Philosophy* 12, pp. 75–93.

Canguilhem, Georges. 1967. "Mort de l'homme ou épuisement du cogito?" *Critique* 24, pp. 599–618.

Carroll, David. 1978. "The Subject of Archaeology; or, The Sovereignty of the Epistēmē." *Modern Language Notes* 93, pp. 695–722.

Certeau, Michel de. 1986. *Heterologies: Discourse on the Other*, trans. Brian Massumi. Minneapolis: University of Minnesota Press.

Comay, Rebecca. 1986. "Excavating the Repressive Hypothesis: Aporias of Liberation in Foucault." *Telos* 67 (Spring), pp. 111–19.

Connolly, William. 1985. "Taylor, Foucault, and Otherness." *Political Theory* 13, no. 3, pp. 365–76.

Cousins, Mark, and Athar Hussain. 1984. *Michel Foucault.* New York: St. Martin's Press.

Deleuze, Gilles. 1970. "Un Nouvel Archiviste." *Critique* 274, pp. 195–209.

———. 1975. "Ecrivain non. Un Nouveau Cartographe." *Critique* 343, pp. 1207–27.

———. 1988. *Foucault* [1986], trans. Sean Hand. Minneapolis: University of Minnesota Press.

Deleuze, Gilles, and Felix Guattari. 1977. *Anti-Oedipus: Capitalism and Schizophrenia* [1972], trans. Robert Hurley, Mark Seem, and Helen R. Lane. New York: Viking Press.

———. 1987. *A Thousand Plateaus* [1980], trans. Brian Massumi. Minneapolis: University of Minnesota Press.

Derrida, Jacques. 1978. "Cogito and the History of Madness" [1967]. In *Writing and Difference*, trans. Alan Bass. Chicago: University of Chicago Press.

Descartes, René. 1927. *Selections*, ed. and trans. Ralph M. Eaton. New York: Charles Scribner's Sons.

———. 1951. *Meditations on First Philosophy* [1641], trans. Laurence J. Lafleur. Indianapolis: Bobbs-Merrill.

Dews, Peter. 1987. *Logics of Disintegration: Post-Structuralist Thought and the Claims of Critical Theory.* London: Verso.

Donzelot, Jacques. 1979. *The Policing of Families* [1977], trans. Robert Hurley. New York: Pantheon Books.

Dreyfus, Hubert L., and Paul Rabinow. 1982. *Michel Foucault: Beyond Structuralism and Hermeneutics.* Chicago: University of Chicago Press.

Felman, Shoshana. 1975. "Madness and Philosophy or Literature's Reason." *Yale French Studies* 52, pp. 206–28.

Foucault, Michel. 1965. *Madness and Civilization: A History of Insanity in the Age of Reason* [1961], trans. Richard Howard. New York: Random House.

———. 1970. *The Order of Things: An Archaeology of the Human Sciences* [1966]. New York: Random House.

———. 1972a. *The Archaeology of Knowledge* [1969] and *The Discourse on Language* [1971], trans. A. M. Sheridan Smith. New York: Harper & Row.

———. 1972b. *Histoire de la folie à l'âge classique.* Paris: Gallimard.

———. 1972c. "History, Discourse, and Discontinuity" [1968], trans. Anthony M. Nazzaro. *Salmagundi* 20 (Summer/Fall), pp. 225–48.

———. 1973. *The Birth of the Clinic: An Archaeology of Medical Perception* [1963], trans. A. M. Sheridan Smith. New York: Vintage Books.

———. 1976a. *Mental Illness and Psychology* [1954], trans. Alan Sheridan. Berkeley: University of California Press.

———. 1976b. "The Politics of Crime," trans. Mollie Horwitz. *Partisan Review* 43, pp. 453–59.

———. 1977a. *Discipline and Punish* [1975], trans. Alan Sheridan. New York: Random House.

———. 1977b. *Language, Counter-Memory, Practice*, ed. Donald F. Bouchard; trans. Donald F. Bouchard and Sherry Simon. Ithaca: Cornell University Press.

———. 1978a. *The History of Sexuality.* Vol. 1: *An Introduction* [1976], trans. Robert Hurley. New York: Random House.

———. 1978b. "Introduction." In Georges Canguilhem, *On the Normal and the Pathological*, trans. Carolyn R. Fawcett. Holland: D. Riedel.

———. 1979. "Governmentality." *I & C* 6, pp. 5–21.

———. 1980a. *Power/Knowledge: Selected Interviews and Other Writings, 1972–1977*, ed. Colin Gordon; trans. Colin Gordon, Leo Marshall, John Mepham, and Kate Soper. New York: Pantheon Books.

———. 1980b. "Truth and Subjectivity." Howison Lecture, presented at University of California–Berkeley.

———. 1981. "Omnes et Singulatim: Toward a Criticism of 'Political Reason.' " In *The Tanner Lectures on Human Values*, vol. 2, ed. Sterling McMurrin. Salt Lake City: University of Utah Press.

———. 1982. "Is It Really Important to Think: An Interview." *Philosophy and Social Criticism* 9, no. 1, pp. 29–40.

———. 1983a. "An Exchange with Michel Foucault." *New York Review of Books*, March 31, 1983, pp. 42–44.

———. 1983b. "Structuralism and Post-Structuralism: An Interview with Michel Foucault," trans. Jeremy Harding. *Telos* 55 (Spring), pp. 195–211.

———. 1984a. "On the Genealogy of Ethics." In *The Foucault Reader*, ed. Paul Rabinow. New York: Pantheon Books.

———. 1984b. "Politics and Ethics: An Interview," trans. Catherine Porter. In *The Foucault Reader*, ed. Paul Rabinow. New York: Pantheon Books.

———. 1984c. "What Is Enlightenment?" trans. Catherine Porter. In *The Foucault Reader*, ed. Paul Rabinow. New York: Pantheon Books.

———. 1985a. "Final Interview" [1984], trans. Thomas Levin and Isabelle Lorenz. *Raritan* 5, no. 1, pp. 1–13.

———. 1985b. *The Use of Pleasure* [1984], trans. Robert Hurley. New York: Pantheon Books.

———. 1986a. *The Care of the Self* [1984], trans. Robert Hurley. New York: Pantheon Books.

———. 1986b. "Dream, Imagination, and Existence" [1954], trans. Forrest Williams. *Review of Existential Psychology & Psychology* 19, no. 1, pp. 29–78.

———. 1986c. "Kant on Enlightenment and Revolution" [1984], trans. Colin Gordon. *Economy and Society* 15, no. 1, pp. 88–96.

———. 1986d. "Nietzsche, Freud, Marx" [1967], trans. Jon Anderson and Gary Hentzi. *Critical Texts* 3, no. 2, pp. 1–5.

———. 1987. "The Thought from Outside" [1966]. In *Foucault/Blanchot*, trans. Jeffrey Mehlman and Brian Massumi. New York: Zone Books.

———. 1988. "Truth, Power, Self: An Interview with Michel Foucault." In *Technologies of the Self*, ed. Luther Martin, Huck Gutman, and Patrick Hutton. Amherst: University of Massachusetts Press.

Fraser, Nancy. 1981. "Foucault on Modern Power: Empirical Insights and Normative Confusions." *Praxis International* 1, no. 3, pp. 272–87.

———. 1985. "Michel Foucault: A 'Young Conservative'?" *Ethics* 96, no. 1, pp. 165–84.

Gandal, Keith. 1986. "Michel Foucault: Intellectual Work and Politics." *Telos* 67 (Spring), pp. 121–34.

Gordon, Colin. 1980. "Afterword." In Michel Foucault, *Power/Knowledge*, ed. Colin Gordon; trans. Colin Gordon, Leo Marshall, John Mepham, and Kate Soper. New York: Pantheon Books.

Grover, Dorothy, Joseph Camp, Jr., and Nuel Belnap, Jr. 1975. "A Prosentential Theory of Truth." *Philosophical Studies* 27, pp. 73–125.

Gutting, Gary. 1989. *Michel Foucault's Archaeology of Scientific Reason*. Cambridge: Cambridge University Press.

Habermas, Jürgen. 1986. "The Genealogical Writing of History: On Some Aporias in Foucault's Theory of Power" [1984], trans. Gregory Ostrander. *Canadian Journal of Political and Social Theory*, 10, nos. 1–2, pp. 1–8.

―――. 1987. *The Philosophical Discourse of Modernity* [1985], trans. Frederick Lawrence. Cambridge: MIT Press.

Hendley, Steven. 1991. "Judgment and Rationality in Lyotard's Discursive Archipelago." *The Southern Journal of Philosophy* 29, no. 2, pp. 227–44.

Hiley, David. 1984. "Foucault and the Analysis of Power: Political Engagement Without Liberal Hope or Comfort." *Praxis International* 4, no. 2, pp. 192–207.

Hobbes, Thomas. 1968. *Leviathan* [1651]. Middlesex: Penguin Books.

Horkheimer, Max, and Theodor W. Adorno. 1972. *Dialectic of Enlightenment* [1944], trans. John Cumming. New York: Seabury Press.

Hoy, David Cousins. 1979. "Taking History Seriously: Foucault, Gadamer, Habermas." *Union Seminary Quarterly Review* 34, no. 2, pp. 85–95.

Hume, David. 1978. *A Treatise of Human Nature* [1740]. Oxford: Clarendon Press.

Huppert, George. 1974. "*Divinatio et Eruditio*: Thoughts on Foucault." *History and Theory* 13, pp. 191–207.

Kant, Immanuel. 1929. *Critique of Pure Reason* [1781–1787], trans. Norman Kemp Smith. New York: St. Martin's Press.

―――. 1963. "What is Enlightenment?" [1784]. In Immanuel Kant, *On History*, ed. and trans. Lewis Beck White. Indianapolis: Bobbs-Merrill.

Keenan, Tom. 1987. "The 'Paradox' of Knowledge and Power: Reading Foucault on a Bias." *Political Theory* 15, no. 1, pp. 5–37.

Lance, Mark, and John Hawthorne. 1990. "From a Normative Point of View." *Pacific Philosophical Quarterly* 71, pp. 28–46.

Lecourt, Dominique. 1975. *Marxism and Epistemology* [1972], trans. Ben Brewster. London: New Left Books.

Leland, Dorothy. 1975. "On Reading and Writing the World: Foucault's History of Thought." *Clio* 4, no. 2, pp. 225–43.

Locke, John. 1980. *Second Treatise of Government* [1690]. Indianapolis: Hackett Publishing.

Lyotard, Jean-François. 1988. *The Differend* [1983], trans. Georges van den Abbeele. Minneapolis: University of Minnesota Press.

Lyotard, Jean-François, and Jean-Loup Thebaud. 1985. *Just Gaming* [1979], trans. Wlad Godzich. Minneapolis: University of Minnesota Press.

McDonnell, Donald. 1977. "On Foucault's Philosophical Method." *Canadian Journal of Philosophy* 7, no. 3, pp. 527–53.

Marx, Karl. 1977. *Capital*, vol. 1 [1867], trans. Ben Fowkes. New York: Vintage Books.

Megill, Allan. 1979. "Foucault, Structuralism, and the Ends of History." *Journal of Modern History* 51 (September), pp. 451–503.

Merquior, J. G. 1985. *Foucault*. Berkeley: University of California Press.

Midelfort, H. C. Erik. 1980. "Madness and Civilization in Early Europe: A Reappraisal of Michel Foucault." In *After the Reformation: Essays in Honor of J.H. Hexter*, ed. B. C. Malament. Philadelphia: University of Pennsylvania Press.

Mill, John Stuart. 1978. *On Liberty* [1859]. Indianapolis: Hackett Publishing.

Minson, Jeffrey. 1980. "Strategies for Socialists? Foucault's Conception of Power." *Economy and Society* 9, no. 1, pp. 1–43.

―――. 1985. *Genealogies of Morals: Nietzsche, Foucault, Donzelot, and the Eccentricity of Ethics*. New York: St. Martin's Press.

Nehamas, Alexander. 1985. *Nietzsche: Life as Literature*. Cambridge: Harvard University Press.

Nietzsche, Friedrich. 1956. *The Birth of Tragedy* [1872] *and The Genealogy of Morals* [1887], trans. Francis Golffing. Garden City: Doubleday.

———. 1967. *The Will to Power* [1901], ed. Walter Kaufman; trans. Walter Kaufman and R. J. Hollingdale. New York: Vintage Books.

Nordquist, Joan. 1986. *Michel Foucault: A Bibliography*. Santa Cruz: Reference and Research Services.

Pasquino, Pasquale. 1986. "Michel Foucault (1926–1984): The Will to Knowledge," trans. Chloe Chard. *Economy and Society* 15, no. 1, pp. 97–109.

Philp, Mark. 1983. "Foucault on Power: A Problem in Radical Translation?" *Political Theory* 11, no. 1, pp. 29–52.

Poster, Mark. 1984. *Foucault, Marxism & History: Mode of Production Versus Mode of Information*. Cambridge: Polity Press.

Poulantzas, Nicos. 1978. *State, Power, Socialism*, trans. Patrick Camiller. London: New Left Books.

Rajchman, John. 1985. *Michel Foucault: The Freedom of Philosophy*. New York: Columbia University Press.

———. 1986. "Ethics After Foucault." *Social Text* 13/14, pp. 165–83.

Ross, Stephen. 1985. "Foucault's Radical Politics." *Praxis International* 5, no. 2, pp. 131–44.

Rousseau, G. S. 1972/73. "Whose Enlightenment? Not Man's: The Case of Foucault." *Eighteenth-Century Studies* 6, pp. 238–56.

Said, Edward. 1978. "The Problem of Textuality: Two Exemplary Positions." *Critical Inquiry* 4, pp. 673–714.

Saussure, Ferdinand de. 1959. *Course in General Linguistics*, ed. Charles Bally and Albert Sechehaye; trans. Wade Baskin. New York: The Philosophical Library.

Sellars, Wilfrid. 1963. "Empiricism and the Philosophy of Mind." In *Science, Perception, and Reality*. London: Routledge & Kegan Paul.

———. 1980. "Inference and Meaning." In *Pure Pragmatics and Possible Worlds*, ed. J. Sicha. Atascadero, Calif.: Ridgeview Publishing.

Sheridan, Alan. 1980. *Michel Foucault: The Will to Truth*. London: Tavistock Publications.

Sluga, Hans. 1985. "Foucault, the Author, and the Discourse." *Inquiry* 28, pp. 403–15.

Smart, Barry. 1983. *Foucault, Marxism, and Critique*. London: Routledge & Kegan Paul.

Spierenenberg, Pieter. 1984. *The Spectacle of Suffering*. Cambridge: Cambridge University Press.

Taylor, Charles. 1986. "Foucault on Freedom and Truth" [1984]. In *Foucault: A Critical Reader*, ed. David Cousins Hoy. Oxford: Basil Blackwell.

Walzer, Michael. 1986. "The Politics of Michel Foucault" [1982]. In *Foucault: A Critical Reader*, ed. David Cousins Hoy. Oxford: Basil Blackwell.

White, Hayden. 1978. "Foucault Decoded: Notes from Underground." In *Tropics of Discourse*. Baltimore: Johns Hopkins University Press.

Wickham, Gary. 1983. "Power and Power Analysis: Beyond Foucault?" *Economy and Society* 12, no. 4, pp. 468–98.

Wittgenstein, Ludwig. 1958. *Philosophical Investigations*, 3rd. ed., trans. G.E.M. Anscombe. New York: Macmillan.

———. 1969. *On Certainty*, ed. G.E.M. Anscombe and G. H. von Wright; trans. Denis Paul and G.E.M. Anscombe. New York: Harper & Row.

———. 1980. *Culture and Value*, ed. G. H. von Wright; trans. Peter Winch. Chicago: University of Chicago Press.

INDEX